1本就通
小學生英文寫作力養成書

全書音檔下載導向頁面

https://globalv.com.tw/mp3-download-9789864544172/

掃描QR碼進入網頁後，按「全書音檔下載請按此」連結，可一次性下載全書音檔壓縮檔，也可點選檔名線上播放。
iOS系統請升級至iOS 13後版本再行下載，此為大型檔案，建議使用WIFI連線下載，以免占用流量，
並請確認連線狀況，以利下載順暢。

前言

大家好，我是孝准老師。

我想問大家一個問題。想要提升擊球技巧的話，就要多加進行打擊練習，想要擁有良好的數學計算能力，就要多做一些計算題。那麼，想要寫好英文作文的話，應該要怎麼做呢？

沒錯，就是多用英文來寫作。

那麼，應該要寫什麼呢？如果寫的是自己的經歷，那麼寫起來會比較輕鬆且內容更自然。所以，最適合用來練習英文寫作的文章就是描寫自身經歷的「日記」。這也是許多老師會強調要用寫日記來練習的原因。

寫英文日記要考慮兩件事。

第一件事就是「要寫什麼內容」。大家每天跟家人、鄰居或朋友之間發生的各種事情就是你的生活經歷，只要如實陳述你的經歷，就能寫出一篇很棒的文章，所以不需要擔心這個問題。

第二件事則是「該如何寫」。

用英文寫句子時，在選擇用「I（我）」做為主詞後，經常會煩惱後面要接哪個動詞才對，這是因為中文裡常會用同一個動詞來表達不同的意義，但英文卻會利用不同的動詞來分別表達這些語意。這裡用下面三個句子來舉例：

① 我看了海。
② 我看了電影。
③ 我看了書。

這三個中文句子都使用了相同的動詞「看了」，可是如果改用英文來寫，那就得用三個不同的動詞來寫這三個句子了。

① I saw the sea.（see：觀看事物或風景）
② I watched a movie.（watch：專注觀看電影）
③ I read a book.（read：閱讀書籍）

中文是一種具有多種修飾詞彙的語言，例如「真的很好」、「超好」、「非常好」、「太好了」和「好極了」全部都是修飾詞彙；然而，英文卻是一種會使用各式各樣動詞來讓語意更加清楚的語言。因此，想要寫好英文作文，就必須明確知道英文動詞的意思才行。

我們在本書中精挑細選出了有出現在英文課本裡、必須好好掌握的動詞單字，詳細說明各個單字所具有的各種語意，並提供了例句，讓大家可以理解該動詞在句中的用法。此外，我們也準備了內有所學動詞的英文句子，讓大家可以理解小短文的內容，繼而寫出屬於自己的精彩文句。剛開始可能連一個句子都很難寫得出來，但只要認真學完這本書，不管是誰都可以成為優秀的英文作家。我們會幫助各位提升英文寫作能力。

Rome was not built in a day. 羅馬不是一天造成的。

鄭苓淮　老師

本書結構與特色

靈活運用做為英文句子核心的各種動詞，透過有趣的方式來練習英文寫作。

1 分鐘小教室
動詞的相關補充說明及易混淆部分的解說。

Step 1 認識核心動詞
仔細理解出現在範文模板中的核心動詞，這裡會透過例句呈現動詞的形態變化及各種語意的實際運用方式。

Step 2 看看別人怎麼寫
好好看過針對當天主題所寫的範文模板，文章中會使用先前所學的核心動詞，並補充其他有出現在範文模板中的詞彙。

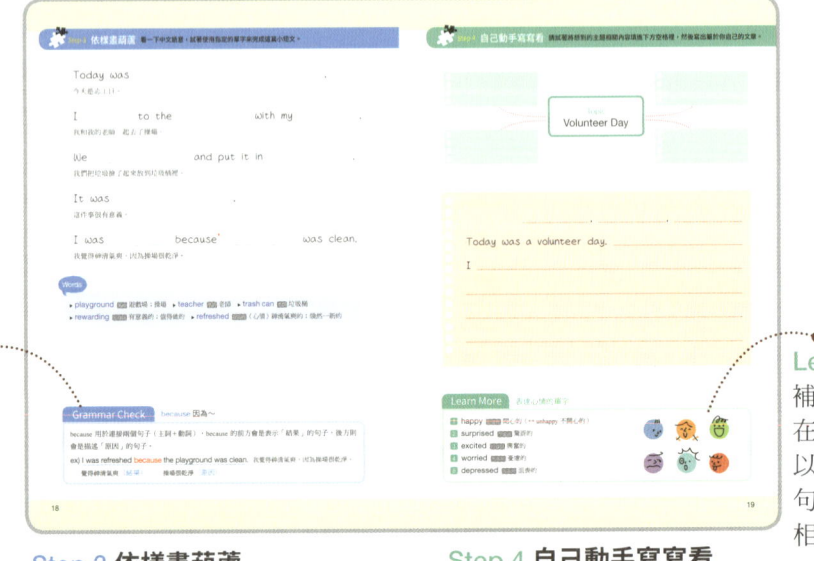

Grammar Check
說明該篇範文模板中一定要知道的文法並補充相關內容。

Learn More
補充說明更多在寫文章時可以使用的詞彙句型或俗語等相關知識。

Step 3 依樣畫葫蘆
利用前面一頁的範文模板，在空格中填入適合的單字來寫出一篇新的短文。

Step 4 自己動手寫寫看
運用前面仔細讀過且練習過的範文句型模板，自己動手寫一篇文章。

Review Test
透過題目檢測與複習當週所學單字、句型和句子。

解答
提供「Step 3 依樣畫葫蘆」與「Review Test」中題目的答案。

動詞形態變化表
利用整理好的表格內容，再次檢視先前所學的全部核心動詞的形態變化。

 **目錄**

前言			2
本書結構與特色			4
動詞的基礎知識			10
英文的基礎知識			12

Week 1

Day 1	Volunteer Day 志工日	go, pick	16	☐ ___月___日
Day 2	P.E. Class 體育課	play, score, win	20	☐ ___月___日
Day 3	Oversleep 睡過頭	wake, hurry, arrive	24	☐ ___月___日
Day 4	Watching Movies 看電影	watch, introduce	28	☐ ___月___日
Day 5	Visiting Grandmother 探望奶奶	visit, bake, smell	32	☐ ___月___日
Review Test 1 (Day 1~5)			36	☐ ___月___日

Week 2

Day 6	Birthday Party 生日派對	invite, come, open	40	☐ ___月___日
Day 7	Meeting Friends 遇到朋友	meet, ask, fail	44	☐ ___月___日
Day 8	Going Skating 去溜冰	go＋V-ing, hold	48	☐ ___月___日
Day 9	Buying a Hat 買帽子	need, buy, change	52	☐ ___月___日
Day 10	Climbing 爬山	climb, grow, drink	56	☐ ___月___日
Review Test 2 (Day 6~10)			60	☐ ___月___日

Week 3

Day 11	School Festival 校慶	dance, sing, record	64	☐ ___月 ___日
Day 12	Borrowing Books 借書	borrow, forget, return	68	☐ ___月 ___日
Day 13	Bad Cold 重感冒	have, wait, take	72	☐ ___月 ___日
Day 14	Catching Dragonflies 抓蜻蜓	fly, try, catch	76	☐ ___月 ___日
Day 15	King Sejong 世宗大王	read, love, die	80	☐ ___月 ___日
Review Test 3 (Day 11~15)			84	☐ ___月 ___日

Week 4

Day 16	Sending a Message 傳訊息	help, send	88	☐ ___月 ___日
Day 17	Flea Market 跳蚤市場	think, sell	92	☐ ___月 ___日
Day 18	Exercise 運動	exercise, start, walk	96	☐ ___月 ___日
Day 19	Discussing Middle School Entrance 討論國中入學的事	become, discuss, agree	100	☐ ___月 ___日
Day 20	Learning Guitar 學吉他	learn, practice, believe	104	☐ ___月 ___日
Review Test 4 (Day 16~20)			108	☐ ___月 ___日

Week 5

Day 21	Boring Day 無聊的日子	feel, call, talk	112	☐	___月___日
Day 22	My Hobby 我的嗜好	collect, listen, turn	116	☐	___月___日
Day 23	Broken Bike 壞掉的腳踏車	paint, take, stay	120	☐	___月___日
Day 24	Congratulations! 恭喜！	congratulate, give, thank	124	☐	___月___日
Day 25	Eat Out 去外面吃	decide, eat, drive	128	☐	___月___日
Review Test 5 (Day 21~25)			132	☐	___月___日

Week 6

Day 26	Go Camping 去露營	cook, sit, see	136	☐	___月___日
Day 27	Stationery Store 文具店	want, pay	140	☐	___月___日
Day 28	Fighting with a Friend 跟朋友吵架	fight, tell, answer	144	☐	___月___日
Day 29	New Sweater 新毛衣	make, look	148	☐	___月___日
Day 30	Math Test 數學測驗	take, study, get	152	☐	___月___日
Review Test 6 (Day 26~30)			156	☐	___月___日

Week 7

Day 31	Doing Housework 做家事	wash, break, say	160	☐ ___月___日
Day 32	Math Study 念數學	understand, cry, solve	164	☐ ___月___日
Day 33	Saving Money 存錢	plan, save, hope	168	☐ ___月___日
Day 34	Moving and Transferring 搬家跟轉學	live, move, miss	172	☐ ___月___日
Day 35	Running 跑步	run, fall, end	176	☐ ___月___日
Review Test 7 (Day 31~35)			180	☐ ___月___日

Week 8

Day 36	Science Museum 科博館	choose, enter, know	184	☐ ___月___日
Day 37	Lie 說謊	hate, lie	188	☐ ___月___日
Day 38	Finding the Wallet 找皮夾	find, clean, remember	192	☐ ___月___日
Day 39	Strengths of My Friend 朋友的優點	have, swim, speak	196	☐ ___月___日
Day 40	Praise 稱讚	draw, show, hang	200	☐ ___月___日
Review Test 8 (Day 36~40)			204	☐ ___月___日

解答 　　　　　　　　　　　　　　　　208
附錄：動詞形態變化表　　　　　　　218

動詞的基礎知識 搶先知道！

※ 動詞的形態

go	去	goes	went	going
① 基本形		② 第三人稱單數現在形	③ 過去形	④ 現在分詞

① 基本形

動詞的原始形態，亦稱作「原形動詞」。在查英文單字時，必須用原形動詞來找。

② 第三人稱*單數現在形

*人稱：表示動作主體，可區分為說話者（第一人稱）、聽者（第二人稱）或第三者（第三人稱）。

○ 第三人稱，指的是排除「我／我們（第一人稱）」、「你／你們（第二人稱）」以外的「第三者（他／他們）」。放在英文來解釋的話，除了 I（我）、We（我們）、You（你／你們）以外，其他人都是第三人稱。 例 He（他）、She（她）、It（它／牠）、They（他們）

○ 單數，指的是「一」。

★ 當主詞是第三人稱單數且時態是現在式時，動詞形態便會產生變化，變化規則如下。

類型	規則	基本形	第三人稱單數現在形
一般動詞	字尾加上 s	make 製造	makes
以 ch／sh／o／x／s 結尾的動詞	字尾加上 es	wash 清洗	washes
字尾是「子音＋y」的動詞	將字尾的 y 換成 i，再加上 es	study 學習	studies
字尾是「母音＋y」的動詞	字尾加上 s	play 玩	plays
have	不規則	have 擁有	has

③ 過去形 描述發生在過去的事件時，必須使用動詞的過去形。從基本形變化為過去形時會遵循下面這些規則。

★ 規則變化

類型	規則	基本形	過去形
一般動詞	字尾加上 ed	want 想要	wanted
		help 幫助	helped
		ask 詢問	asked
		look 注視	looked

以 e 結尾的動詞	字尾加上 d	like 喜歡	like**d**
		love 喜愛	love**d**
		hope 希望	hope**d**
		surprise 使吃驚	surprise**d**
以「子音＋y」結尾的動詞	將字尾的 y 換成 i，再加上 ed	cry 哭泣	cr**ied**
		hurry 趕緊	hurr**ied**
以「短母音＋短子音」結尾的動詞	將字尾的子音再重複一次，然後加上 ed	stop 停止	stop**ped**
		plan 計劃	plan**ned**

★ 不規則變化

基本形	過去形	基本形	過去形
come 來	came	go 去	went
eat 吃	ate	drink 喝	drank
see 看	saw	meet 見面	met
say 說	said	do 做	did
tell 告訴	told	draw 畫	drew

在英文動詞中，過去形是不規則變化的動詞非常多，因此與其想著要一口氣全部背起來，不如遇到一個背一個。

④ 現在分詞

描述現在正在進行中的動作或狀態。在句子裡會以「基本形＋ing」的形態出現，可以扮演的功能角色十分多樣化。

英文的基礎知識 搶先知道！

※ 日期、星期與天氣的寫法

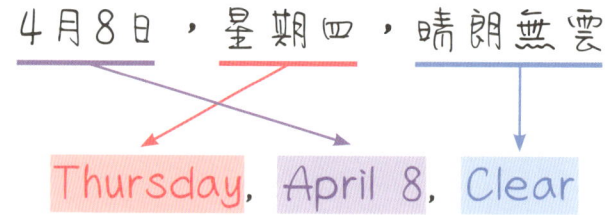

○ 用英文寫日期跟星期時，順序是「星期, 月＋日」。
○ 「星期」與「月＋日」之間會用逗號（,）連接，逗號後面要空半格才接「月＋日」，「星期」的字首要大寫。
○ 「日」後面先接逗號（,），空半格後再描述「天氣」，天氣的字首也要大寫。

星期 Day　*可用（）的縮寫來表示。

星期一	Monday (Mon.)	星期五	Friday (Fri.)
星期二	Tuesday (Tues.)	星期六	Saturday (Sat.)
星期三	Wednesday (Wed.)	星期日	Sunday (Sun.)
星期四	Thursday (Thur.)		

月份 Month　*可用（）的縮寫來表示。

1月	January (Jan.)	7月	July (Jul.)
2月	February (Feb.)	8月	August (Aug.)
3月	March (Mar.)	9月	September (Sep.)
4月	April (Apr.)	10月	October (Oct.)
5月	May	11月	November (Nov.)
6月	June (Jun.)	12月	December (Dec.)

日 Date

*日期用數字或序數來呈現都可以，但讀的時候都要用序數的唸法來讀。

1 日	1st (first)	11 日	11th (eleventh)	21 日	21st (twenty-first)
2 日	2nd (second)	12 日	12th (twelfth)	22 日	22nd (twenty-second)
3 日	3rd (third)	13 日	3th (thirteenth)	23 日	23rd (twenty-third)
4 日	4th (fourth)	14 日	14th (fourteenth)	24 日	24th (twenty-fourth)
5 日	5th (fifth)	15 日	15th (fifteenth)	...	
6 日	6th (sixth)	16 日	16th (sixteenth)	30 日	30th (thirtieth)
7 日	7th (seventh)	17 日	17th (seventeenth)	31 日	31st (thirty-first)
8 日	8th (eighth)	18 日	18th (eighteenth)		
9 日	9th (ninth)	19 日	19th (nineteenth)		
10 日	10th (tenth)	20 日	20th (twentieth)		

天氣 Weather

晴朗無雲的	clear	多雲的	cloudy
溫暖的	warm	下雨的	rainy
晴朗的	sunny	暴風雨的	stormy
涼爽的	cool	起霧的	foggy
颳風的	windy	冷颼颼的	chilly
炎熱的	hot	寒冷的	cold
潮濕的	humid	下雪的	snowy
濕熱的	sticky	極冷的	freezing

Week 1

Day 1 **go, pick** ▸ 志工日

Day 2 **play, score, win** ▸ 體育課

Day 3 **wake, hurry, arrive** ▸ 睡過頭

Day 4 **watch, introduce** ▸ 看電影

Day 5 **visit, bake, smell** ▸ 探望奶奶

Review Test 1

Day 1

Volunteer Day 志工日

Step 1 認識核心動詞

go	去	goes	went	going
		第三人稱單數現在形	過去形	現在分詞

 1 分鐘小教室

go 是用來描述「從某一個地點移動到另一個地點」的動詞。go 會在即將「遠離說話對象」的情況下使用，如果是「即將靠近說話對象」的情況，則必須使用 come。舉例來說，跟朋友通電話時若說：「我正在去的路上」，因為描述的是「自己離說話對象的距離越來越近」，所以英文必須說「I'm coming.」才對。

▨ （從一個地點移動到其他地點）去：**go＋to＋目的地**

　I **go to school** at 8 o'clock. 我 8 點鐘去上學。

▨ **go** vs. **come**

　I'll **go** home early.
　（和朋友告別時說）我會早點回家。
　I'll **come** home early.
　（和媽媽通電話時說）我會早點回家。

pick	① 挑選；選擇 ② 摘 ② 撿	picks	picked	picking
		第三人稱單數現在形	過去形	現在分詞

▨ 挑選；選擇

　Pick a number from one to ten. 從 1 到 10 中選擇一個數字。

▨ 摘（花或果實）

　I **picked** an apple yesterday. 我昨天摘了一個蘋果。

▨ 撿：**pick up**

　They **picked up** the trash. 他們撿了垃圾。

16

 Step 2　**看看別人怎麼寫**　請邊聽音檔邊仔細看過一遍，接著再重新唸一遍。

Monday, March 12, Warm

Today was a volunteer day.

I went to the park with my classmates.

We picked up the trash and put it in the trash bag.

It was hard.

However, I was happy because the park was clean.

今天是志工日。
我和我的同學們一起去了公園。
我們把垃圾撿起來放進了垃圾袋裡。
這件事很辛苦。
不過，我很開心，因為公園變乾淨了。

Words

▸ volunteer 名詞 志工 動詞 自願做（某件事）　▸ classmate 名詞 同班同學　▸ trash 名詞 垃圾
▸ hard 形容詞 辛苦的；堅硬的　▸ however 副詞 不過，然而　▸ because 連接詞 因為

Step 3 **依樣畫葫蘆** 看一下中文語意，試著使用指定的單字來完成這篇小短文。

Today was _____.
今天是志工日。

I _____ to the _____ with my _____.
我和我的老師一起去了操場。

We _____ and put it in _____.
我們把垃圾撿了起來放到垃圾桶裡。

It was _____.
這件事很有意義。

I was _____ because* _____ was clean.
我覺得神清氣爽，因為操場很乾淨。

Words

- **playground** 名詞 遊戲場；操場 ▶ **teacher** 名詞 老師 ▶ **trash can** 名詞 垃圾桶
- **rewarding** 形容詞 有意義的；值得做的 ▶ **refreshed** 形容詞 （心情）神清氣爽的；煥然一新的

Grammar Check because 因為～

because 用於連接兩個句子（主詞＋動詞），because 的前方會是表示「結果」的句子，後方則會是描述「原因」的句子。

ex) I was refreshed **because** the playground was clean.　我覺得神清氣爽，因為操場很乾淨。
　　　覺得神清氣爽（結果）　　操場很乾淨（原因）

18

Step 4 自己動手寫寫看
請試著將想到的主題相關內容填進下方空格裡，然後寫出屬於你自己的文章。

Topic
Volunteer Day

..................., ..., ...

Today was a volunteer day.

I ....

....

....

....

Learn More　表達「心情」的單字

1. happy 形容詞 開心的（↔ unhappy 不開心的）
2. surprised 形容詞 驚訝的
3. excited 形容詞 興奮的
4. worried 形容詞 憂慮的
5. depressed 形容詞 沮喪的

Day 2　P.E. Class 體育課

🧩 Step 1　認識核心動詞

play	① 玩耍 ② （和～）比賽； 　　進行（遊戲或運動） ③ 演奏	plays 第三人稱單數現在形	played 過去形	playing 現在分詞

1 分鐘小教室

play 常用來描述「進行某項運動」或「玩耍」，但也可用來表達「演奏樂器」的意思。此外，想描述在戲劇或電影中負責扮演某一角色時，也會用 play 這個字。

▨ （拿著～）玩：**play**（with＋物品）
　We **played** with Legos.　我們玩了樂高。

▨ （和～）比賽；進行（遊戲或運動）：**play**＋項目（with 對象）
　I **played baseball** with my father yesterday.
　我昨天和爸爸一起打了棒球。

▨ 演奏：**play**＋**the**＋樂器
　Can you **play the piano**?　你會彈鋼琴嗎？
　＊樂器名稱的前面通常要加上 the。

score	得分	scores 第三人稱單數現在形	scored 過去形	scoring 現在分詞

▨ 得分：**score**＋分數（in＋項目）
　He **scored 2 points** in basketball.　他在打籃球時得了兩分。
　Tip score 也可做為名詞，表示「得分」或「分數」。
　　My math *score* is 90.　我的數學分數是 90 分。

win	贏得；獲勝	wins 第三人稱單數現在形	won 過去形	winning 現在分詞

▨ 贏得；獲勝：**win**＋比賽
　Our team **won the baseball game**.　我們隊贏得了棒球比賽。
　Tip lose：（在比賽中）輸掉；遺失（物品）＊過去形是 lost
　　We *lost* the badminton game.　我們輸掉了羽球比賽。

20

 Step 2 **看看別人怎麼寫** 請邊聽音檔邊仔細看過一遍，接著再重新唸一遍。

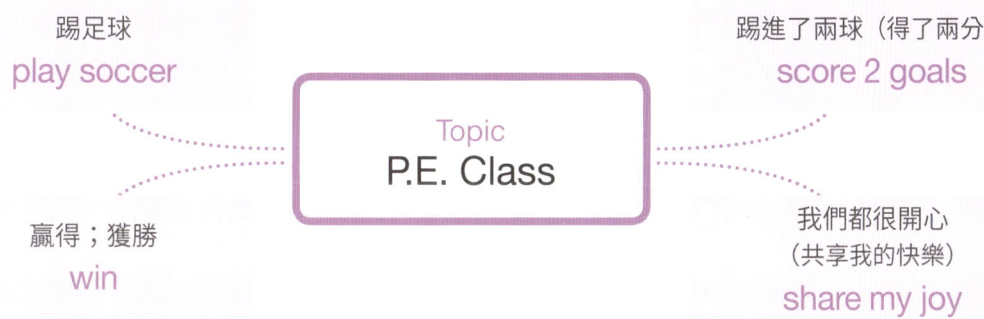

Tuesday, April 14, Windy

I played soccer with my friends in P.E. class.

I scored 2 goals in the second half.

It was a close game, but my team won.

I shared my joy with my friends.

Hard work pays off.

　　　　　　　　　　我在體育課時跟朋友們一起踢了足球。
　　　　　　　　　　我在下半場踢進了兩球（得了兩分）。
　　　　　　　　　　這是一場很接近的比賽，但我們隊贏了。
　　　　　　　　　　我和朋友們都很開心。
　　　　　　　　　　（英文俗語）努力付出就會有收穫。

Words

- P.E.(physical education) class 體育課　▶ second half 下半場
- a close game 一場很接近的比賽　▶ share 動詞 分享；共享　▶ work 名詞 工作；努力
- pay off 有收穫，得到好結果

Step 3 依樣畫葫蘆　看一下中文語意，試著使用指定的單字來完成這篇小短文。

I _____ with my friends in* _____.
我在體育課時跟朋友們一起打了籃球。

I _____ 2 goals in the _____.
我在上半場進了兩球。

It was _____, but my team _____.
這是一場很接近的比賽，但我們隊贏了。

I _____ with joy.
我高興地大叫。

_____
（英文俗語）努力付出就會有收穫。

Words

▶ basketball 名詞 籃球　▶ first half 上半場　▶ shout 動詞 大喊，大叫

Grammar Check　　in 在～之內

in 表示「在～時間或空間之內」的概念。因為是在體育課的「上課時間之內（in）」進行體育活動，所以英文會說成 in P.E. Class。如果想說「他在辦公室」，則表示某人在「名為辦公室的空間之內」，所以英文說法會是 He is in the office.。

22

Step 4　自己動手寫寫看　請試著將想到的主題相關內容填進下方空格裡，然後寫出屬於你自己的文章。

Topic
P.E. Class

_____, _____,

I played _____ in P.E. class. _____

_____

_____

_____

_____

Learn More　跟「努力」有關的英文俗語

1. **No pains, no gains.** 沒有付出就沒有收穫。
   *pain 名詞 痛苦；疼痛　gain 名詞 收穫，獲得
2. **Slow and steady win the game.** 欲速則不達。（緩慢且穩定者贏得比賽）
   *steady 形容詞 穩定的

Day 3　Oversleep 睡過頭

 Step 1　認識核心動詞

wake	① 清醒；醒來 ② 喚醒	wakes 第三人稱單數現在形	woke 過去形	waking 現在分詞

 1分鐘小教室

wake up 跟 get up 是語意相近的慣用表達方式，但兩者的語意仍略有不同。wake up 描述的是「剛張開眼睛醒來」的狀態，get up 則是「睡醒並起身」的動作。

▨ （從睡夢中）清醒；醒來：**wake up**

He wakes up early. 他很早醒。

▨ 喚醒：**wake＋對象＋up**

Every day my mom wakes me up.
我媽媽每天都會叫醒我。

hurry	趕緊；匆忙	hurries 第三人稱單數現在形	hurried 過去形	hurrying 現在分詞

▨ 趕緊；匆忙

Hurry up! 快點！

▨ 趕緊地，匆忙地：**in a hurry**

I had lunch in a hurry. 我匆忙地吃了午餐。

arrive	抵達	arrives 第三人稱單數現在形	arrived 過去形	arriving 現在分詞

▨ 抵達（某地點）：**arrive＋at＋地點**（範圍較小的地點或建築物）

I arrived at the library. 我抵達了圖書館。

▨ 抵達（某地點）：**arrive＋in＋地點**（範圍較為寬闊的地點）

I arrived in Seoul yesterday. 我昨天抵達了首爾。

 **Step 2** 看看別人怎麼寫　請邊聽音檔邊仔細看過一遍，接著再重新唸一遍。

Wednesday, August 12, Hot

I woke up late in the morning.

I didn't hear the alarm.

I hurried to school without eating breakfast.

I arrived at school after the first period.

I quietly entered the classroom through the back door.

我今天早上睡太晚了。
我沒有聽到鬧鐘響。
我沒吃早餐就趕緊去了學校。
我在過了第一節課之後才到學校。
我從後門安靜地進了教室。

Words

▶ oversleep 動詞 睡過頭　▶ period 名詞 （一節）課；一段期間　▶ quietly 副詞 安靜地，平靜地
▶ enter 動詞 進入　▶ classroom 名詞 教室　▶ through 介系詞 藉由～

Step 3 **依樣畫葫蘆** 看一下中文語意，試著使用指定的單字來完成這篇小短文。

I _____ late in the _____.
我今天早上睡太晚了。

I didn't _____.
我沒有聽到鬧鐘響。

I _____ school without* _____.
我臉都沒洗就趕緊去了學校。

I _____ school after the _____.
我在過了第二節課之後才到學校。

I quietly entered the classroom through the _____.
我從前門安靜地進了教室。

Words

▸ wash 動詞 清洗　▸ face 名詞 臉　▸ second 形容詞 第二個的　▸ front 形容詞 前面的；正面的

Grammar Check　without 沒有～

without 後面必須接名詞，所以如果要接有用到動詞的表達用語，就必須先將動詞名詞化成動名詞（V-ing）才行。

ex) **without** food 沒有食物
　　without saying goodbye 沒有說再見

Step 4　自己動手寫寫看　請試著將想到的主題相關內容填進下方空格裡，然後寫出屬於你自己的文章。

Topic
Oversleep

..................,　..................,　..................

I woke up late in the morning.

Learn More　表示事物順序的數字（序數）ex) 名次、級數、學年、日期、建築物樓層等等

1　第一　first
2　第二　second
3　第三　third
4　第四　fourth
5　第五　fifth
6　第六　sixth
7　第七　seventh
8　第八　eighth
9　第九　ninth
10　第十　tenth

Day 4 Watching Movies 看電影

Step 1 認識核心動詞

watch	① 觀看；注視 ② 警戒	watches 第三人稱單數現在形	watched 過去形	watching 現在分詞

1分鐘小教室

watch 主要用來描述「觀看會移動的對象」，因為電視或電影畫面中出現的人事物也被視為會移動的對象，所以描述看電視或看電影時要用 watch。另一方面，圖片（picture）不會移動，所以描述「看圖片」時要用 look 這個動詞。
Look at the picture.
請看這張圖片。

▧ 觀看；注視
He watches TV for an hour every day.
他每天會看一個小時的電視。

▧ 警戒：watch out（for＋對象）
Watch out for the cars.
小心看車。

 Tip watch 也可做為名詞，意思是「手錶」。
Whose watch is this? 這是誰的手錶？

introduce	① 介紹 ② 推出	introduces 第三人稱單數現在形	introduced 過去形	introducing 現在分詞

▧ （向～）介紹～：introduce＋要介紹的對象＋to＋接受介紹的對象

Let me introduce myself to you.
讓我來（向你們）自我介紹一下吧。

▧ （向～）推出～：introduce＋商品＋to＋市場（消費者）

Samsung Electronics introduced a new mobile phone to the market.
三星電子（向市場）推出了一款新手機。

28

Step 2 看看別人怎麼寫　請邊聽音檔邊仔細看過一遍，接著再重新唸一遍。

Wednesday, December 12, Cold

I watched the movie *Frozen* with my mom.

I ate popcorn while watching the movie.

The movie was so fun.

Two hours passed quickly.

I will introduce the movie to my friends tomorrow.

我和媽媽一起看了電影《冰雪奇緣》。
我看電影的時候吃了爆米花。
這部電影非常有趣。
兩個小時過得很快。
我明天會向我的朋友們介紹這部電影。

Words

- ate 動詞 吃（eat 的過去形）
- while 連接詞 當～的時候
- so 副詞 那麼，非常
- pass 動詞 經過
- quickly 副詞 快速地
- tomorrow 副詞 明天

29

Step 3 依樣畫葫蘆　看一下中文語意，試著使用指定的單字來完成這篇小短文。

I _____ the movie Spider-Man with my _____.
我和姊姊一起看了電影《蜘蛛人》。

I ate _____ while* watching the movie.
我在看電影時吃了洋芋片。

The movie was _____.
這部電影很讓人緊張。

_____ passed quickly.
兩個半小時過得很快。

I will _____ the movie _____ my _____ tomorrow.
我明天會向我的朋友們介紹這部電影。

Words
- potato chips（切成薄片的）炸馬鈴薯，洋芋片
- tense 形容詞 緊張的；令人緊張的；緊繃的
- two and a half hours 兩個半小時

Grammar Check　while 當～的時候

while 用來描述「兩種情況在同一時間發生」。句型為「A（主詞＋動詞）while B（主詞＋動詞）」，表示「在做 B 時發生了 A」。若 A 跟 B 的主詞相同，則 B 必須省略主詞並改寫成「while＋V-ing」。

ex) I ate potato chips while watching the movie. 我在看電影時吃了洋芋片。
　　　　A　　　　　　　　B

*A 跟 B 的主詞相同，所以變成「while＋（主詞省略）＋watching」。

 **Step 4 自己動手寫寫看**　請試著將想到的主題相關內容填進下方空格裡，然後寫出屬於你自己的文章。

Topic
Watching Movies

..................., ..., ...
I watched the movie ....

Learn More　電影類型

1. comic movie 漫畫改編電影
2. horror movie 恐怖電影
3. thriller movie 驚悚電影 *令人感到緊張不安的電影
4. action movie 動作電影 *以角色的武打、特技表演等內容為主的電影
5. romance movie 浪漫電影

Day 5 Visiting Grandmother 探望奶奶

Step 1 認識核心動詞

visit	① 探望；拜訪 ② 訪問（網站等）	visits 第三人稱單數現在形	visited 過去形	visiting 現在分詞

▧ 探望；拜訪

I will **visit** my uncle tomorrow.　我明天會去探望我的叔叔。

▧ 訪問（網站等）

For more information, **visit** our website.
如果需要更多資訊，請上我們的網站。

bake	烘焙（麵包等）	bakes 第三人稱單數現在形	baked 過去形	baking 現在分詞

1 分鐘小教室

描述「烘焙」時用 bake，描述在油裡「煎炒炸」時要用 fry。用烤箱或火來「炙烤」時，則要用 roast。

▧ 烘焙（麵包等）

Bake bread in the oven for 5 minutes.
將麵包放入烤箱內烤 5 分鐘。

Tip　烘焙麵包的店稱作 bakery，
　　 烘焙麵包的人則稱作 baker。

smell	① 發出味道 ② 聞味道	smells 第三人稱單數現在形	smelled 過去形	smelling 現在分詞

▧ 發出（特定的）味道：**smell**＋味道／香氣

The flower **smells** fragrant.　這花散發出香氣。

▧ 聞味道：**smell**＋發出味道的對象

She **smelled** the scent of roses.　她聞到了玫瑰花的香味。

32

Step 2　看看別人怎麼寫　請邊聽音檔邊仔細看過一遍，接著再重新唸一遍。

MP3-005

每個禮拜去看
visit every week

烤麵包
bake the bread

Topic
Visiting Grandmother

聞起來真的很香
smell really good

超好吃
taste amazing

Saturday, November 19, Cold

I visit my grandmother every week.

Last week, she baked bread.

It smelled really good.

I ate a loaf of bread, and it tasted amazing.

My grandmother smiled happily.

我每個禮拜都會去看奶奶。
上個禮拜她烤了麵包。
麵包聞起來真的很香。
我吃了一條麵包，超好吃。
我奶奶開心地微笑。

Words

▶ every week 每個禮拜　▶ last 形容詞 上一個的；最後的　▶ a loaf of（麵包等）一條或一塊的
▶ taste 動詞 嚐起來；有～的味道　▶ amazing 形容詞 驚人的，令人驚豔的

33

Step 3 依樣畫葫蘆　看一下中文語意，試著使用指定的單字來完成這篇小短文。

I _____ my grandmother _____.
我每個月都會去看奶奶。

_____, she _____.
上個月她烤了一個派。

It _____ really good.
派聞起來真的很香。

I ate* _____, and it tasted _____.
我吃了一塊派，吃起來很甜。

My grandmother _____ happily.
我的奶奶開心地微笑。

Words
▶ month 名詞 月　▶ pie 名詞 派，餡餅　▶ a piece of 一塊的　▶ sweet 形容詞 甜的

Grammar Check　動詞的不規則過去形

一般而言，動詞的過去形就是在基本形的字尾加上 ed，但也有許多動詞的變化方式不會照著一般規則走，例如 ate（eat 的過去形）。與其想要一口氣背完所有的動詞不規則變化，倒不如將新出現在句子中的動詞不規則變化一個一個記下來就好。

ex) go 去 → went 去了　buy 買 → bought 買了　put 放 → put 放了

Step 4　自己動手寫寫看　請試著將想到的主題相關內容填進下方空格裡，然後寫出屬於你自己的文章。

Topic
Visiting _____

_____, _____,

I visit(ed) _____

Learn More　親戚（relative）

1. grandfather 爺爺；外公
2. uncle 叔叔；伯伯；舅舅
3. aunt 阿姨；姑姑；嬸嬸
4. cousin 堂表兄弟姊妹
5. nephew 外甥；姪子
6. niece 外甥女；姪女

35

Review Test 1　(Day 1~5)

A　請寫出與以下中文相對應的英文動詞。

1. 探望；拜訪；訪問（網站等）　→　visit
2. 趕緊；匆忙　→　h_____
3. 得分　→　s_____
4. 去　→　g_____
5. 發出味道；聞味道　→　s_____
6. 觀看；注視；警戒　→　w_____
7. 清醒；醒來；喚醒　→　w_____
8. 玩耍；（和～）比賽；進行（遊戲或運動）；演奏　→　p_____
9. 介紹；推出　→　i_____
10. 挑選；選擇；摘；撿　→　p_____
11. 贏得；獲勝　→　w_____
12. 抵達　→　a_____
13. 烘焙（麵包等）　→　b_____

B　請將英文單字與相對應的中文字義連起來。

1. classmate　　　　　ⓐ 分享；共享
2. quietly　　　　　　ⓑ （麵包等）一條或一塊的
3. amazing　　　　　ⓒ 同班同學
4. share　　　　　　ⓓ 安靜地，平靜地
5. while　　　　　　ⓔ 明天
6. a loaf of　　　　　ⓕ 睡過頭
7. however　　　　　ⓖ 工作；努力
8. oversleep　　　　　ⓗ 驚人的，令人驚豔的
9. tomorrow　　　　　ⓘ 當～的時候
10. work　　　　　　ⓙ 不過，然而

36

C 請根據中文句意將適當的字詞填入空格之中，完成英文句子。

1. We　picked up the trash　and put it in the _____.
   我們把垃圾撿了起來放進垃圾桶裡。

2. I _____ 2 goals in the _____.
   我在上半場進了兩球。

3. I _____ late in the _____.
   我今天早上睡太晚了。

4. _____ passed quickly.
   兩個半小時過得很快。

5. I ate _____ bread and it tasted _____.
   我吃了一片麵包，吃起來很甜。

D 請利用下列提示的英文動詞來寫出符合中文句意的英文句子。

1. go　　　　I went to the park with my classmates.
   我和同學們一起去了公園。

2. play　　　_____
   我在體育課時跟朋友們一起踢了足球。

3. hurry　　 _____
   我沒吃早餐就趕緊去了學校。

4. introduce　_____
   我明天會向我的朋友們介紹這部電影。

5. visit　　　_____
   我每個禮拜都會去探望奶奶。

37

Week 2

Day 6 **invite, come, open** ▸ 生日派對

Day 7 **meet, ask, fail** ▸ 遇到朋友

Day 8 **go＋V-ing, hold** ▸ 去溜冰

Day 9 **need, buy, change** ▸ 買帽子

Day 10 **climb, grow, drink** ▸ 爬山

Review Test 2

Day 6　Birthday Party 生日派對

Step 1　認識核心動詞

invite	邀請	invite**s**	invite**d**	invit**ing**
		第三人稱單數現在形	過去形	現在分詞

▨ 邀請：**invite＋對象＋to＋活動／地點**

　She **invited** me to dinner.　她邀請了我去吃晚餐。

　Tip invite 的名詞是 invitation，除了表示「邀請」這件事之外，也可用來表示「邀請函」。

come	來	come**s**	**came**	com**ing**
		第三人稱單數現在形	過去形	現在分詞

1 分鐘小教室

就像在 Day 1 學到的一樣，come 表達的是「正朝著說話對象前進」的意思。在 Day 3 中學到的 arrive，意思是「抵達『某個目的地』」，come 則是「朝著某個方向前進，『無論最終是否抵達目的地』」。

▨ 來～：**come＋to＋地點**

　Can you **come to** my house today?
　你今天可以來我家嗎？

▨ 來做～：**come＋to＋動詞**

　He **comes to see** me every week.
　他每個禮拜都來看我。

open	① 打開～ ② 開	open**s**	open**ed**	open**ing**
		第三人稱單數現在形	過去形	現在分詞

▨ 打開～：**open**

　I **opened** the door and went inside.　我打開了門進去裡面。

▨ 開

　The wind blew and the door **opened**.　風吹過後門開了。

Step 2 看看別人怎麼寫 請邊聽音檔邊仔細看過一遍，接著再重新唸一遍。

11 歲生日
11th birthday

邀請朋友
invite friends

Topic
Birthday Party

生日禮物
birthday present

覺得感動的
touched

Thursday, February 12, Cold

Today was my 11th birthday.

I invited friends to my birthday party.

They came to my house on time.

They prepared a present for my birthday.

I opened it. It was a nice wallet.

I was touched.

今天是我的 11 歲生日。
我邀請了朋友們來我的生日派對。
他們準時來到了我家。
他們準備了一份生日禮物給我。
我打開了禮物。是個很棒的皮夾。
我覺得很感動。

Words

- **on time** 準時，按時
- **prepare** 動詞 準備，籌備
- **present** 名詞 禮物
- **wallet** 名詞 皮夾
- **touched** 形容詞 覺得感動的，被打動的

Step 3 依樣畫葫蘆 看一下中文語意，試著使用指定的單字來完成這篇小短文。

Today was my 11th* _____.
今天是我的 11 歲生日。

I _____ friends _____ my birthday party.
我邀請了朋友們來我的生日派對。

They came to my house _____.
他們晚了 30 分鐘才來到我家。

They _____ a present for my birthday.
他們準備了一份生日禮物給我。

I _____ it. It was a nice _____.
我打開了禮物。是個很棒的鉛筆盒。

I was _____ it.
我很滿意這個鉛筆盒。

Words

▶ minute 名詞（時間單位）分鐘　▶ late 副詞 遲到；晚　▶ pencil case 名詞 鉛筆盒
▶ satisfied with 對～感到滿意

Grammar Check　序數的數字寫法

我們在 Day 3 曾學過序數，當想以數字來表示序數時，必須在數字之後緊接 -st、-nd 或 -th 這幾個字尾。

first	1st	tenth	10th
second	2nd	eleventh	11th
third	3rd	twelfth	12th

42

Step 4　自己動手寫寫看　請試著將想到的主題相關內容填進下方空格裡，然後寫出屬於你自己的文章。

Topic
Birthday Party

..................., ..., ...

Today was my ....th birthday. ....

....

....

....

....

Learn More　　單字小故事 ❶ pre（前；預先）

單字開頭的 pre 具有「前」和「預先」的意思。例如 present 其實是「前（pre）＋送出（sent＝send）」，表示「送到某人的面前」，用來傳達「出現」或是「送禮物給某人」的意思，所以 present 也有著「出席的」和「禮物」這兩種意思。prepare 的組成則是「預先（pre）＋準備（pare）」，所以具有「準備；籌備」的意思。組成 preview 的則是「預先（pre）＋看（view）」，所以有著「預看」和「試映」的意思。

43

Day 7　Meeting Friends 遇到朋友

Step 1　認識核心動詞

meet	遇到；碰面	**meets** 第三人稱單數現在形	**met** 過去形	**meeting** 現在分詞

▧ 遇到：**meet＋對象**

Where did you meet her?　你在哪裡遇到她的？

▧ 碰面

We meet every week.　我們每個禮拜都會碰面。

ask	① 問；詢問 ② 要求；請求	**asks** 第三人稱單數現在形	**asked** 過去形	**asking** 現在分詞

▧ （向～）問；詢問（關於～）：**ask＋對象＋about＋內容**

I asked him about his vacation schedule.
我詢問他有關他的假期安排的事。

▧ （向～）要求；請求（去做～）：**ask＋對象＋to＋動詞**

I asked him to close the window.
我請他去關窗戶。

fail	（在考試中） 沒有通過或 不及格；失敗	**fails** 第三人稱單數現在形	**failed** 過去形	**failing** 現在分詞

▧ （在考試中）沒有通過或不及格

She failed her driving test.　她考駕照沒過。

▧ 失敗：**fail＋in＋試圖達成的事項**（或領域）

He failed in business.　他經商失敗了。

Step 2 看看別人怎麼寫 請邊聽音檔邊仔細看過一遍，接著再重新唸一遍。

在我去 Jane 家的路上
on my way to Jane's house

遇到 Min-su
meet Min-su

Topic
Meeting Friends

考試不及格
fail the test

鼓勵
encourage

Thursday, April 28, Clear

On my way to Jane's house, I met Min-su on the street.

Min-su looked in a bad mood.

I asked him, "How are you?"

He said, "I failed the computer certification test."

I encouraged him.

在我去 Jane 家的路上，我在街上遇到了 Min-su。
Min-su 看起來心情很不好。
我問他：「你好嗎？」
他說：「我的電腦檢定考沒過。」
我鼓勵了他。

Words

- street 名詞 街道
- mood 名詞 心情，情緒
- certification 名詞 檢定；證明
- encourage 動詞 鼓勵；促進

Step 3 依樣畫葫蘆　看一下中文語意，試著使用指定的單字來完成這篇小短文。

On my way to _____, I _____ Min-su on*
_____.

在我去才藝班的路上，我在街上遇到了 Min-su。

Min-su looked in a _____.

Min-su 看起來心情很不好。

I _____ him, "How are you?"

我問他：「你好嗎？」

He said, "I _____ the _____ exam."

他說：「我的韓國史考不及格。」

I _____ him.

我安慰了他。

Words

▶ **academy** 名詞（特定領域的）學院；才藝班　▶ **history** 名詞 歷史　▶ **exam** 名詞 測驗，考試
▶ **comfort** 動詞 安慰

Grammar Check　on 在～之上

on 的語意帶有「接觸」之意，所以接觸著路面（在路面之上）的無論是車子還是人，英文的說法都是 on the street。將蘋果放在桌面上時，因為蘋果跟桌子之間相互接觸，所以英文會說成 An apple is on the table。

46

Step 4　自己動手寫寫看　請試著將想到的主題相關內容填進下方空格裡，然後寫出屬於你自己的文章。

Topic
Meeting Friends

_____, _____, _____

I met _____

_____

_____

_____

Learn More　跟「失敗」和「成功」有關的名言

Success is walking from failure to failure with no loss of enthusiasm.
成功就是經歷一次次的失敗，仍不減熱忱。

— Winston S. Churchill —

*success 名詞 成功　　failure 名詞 失敗　　enthusiasm 名詞 熱情，熱忱

47

Day 8　Going Skating 去溜冰

Step 1　認識核心動詞

go ＋V-ing	去做～	goes＋V-ing	went＋V-ing	going＋V-ing
		第三人稱單數現在形	過去形	現在分詞

1 分鐘小教室

在 Day1 我們曾學過 go 的意思是「去」，而在 go 的後面緊接 V-ing 時，語意就會變成「去做～」。「go＋V-ing」只會用來描述「從事某項運動或休閒活動」。另一方面，請記得英文中沒有「go to＋動詞」這種表達方式。
I go shopping at the market.
I go to shop at the market. (X)

▨ 去做～

go skating 去溜冰
go skiing 去滑雪
go camping 去露營
go hiking 去健行
go swimming 去游泳
go shopping 去購物
go jogging 去慢跑
I went fishing with my dad last week.
我上個禮拜跟爸爸一起去釣了魚。

hold	① 握著；抓住 ② 保持	holds	held	holding
		第三人稱單數現在形	過去形	現在分詞

▨ 握著；抓住

I held the pen tightly. 我緊緊握著筆。

▨ 保持：hold on

Hold on, please. 請（保持電話不要掛斷）稍等。
Can you hold on for a minute? 可以請你（保持電話不要掛斷）稍待片刻嗎？

Step 2 看看別人怎麼寫 請邊聽音檔邊仔細看過一遍，接著再重新唸一遍。

和家人一起
with my family

第一次
first time

Topic
Going Skating

小心翼翼地移動
move cautiously

緊張的
nervous

Sunday, January 2, Cold

I went skating with my family.

It was my first time skating.

The ice floor was slippery.

I held my father's hand.

I moved forward cautiously. I was nervous and sweated a lot.

我和家人一起去溜冰了。
這是我第一次溜冰。
冰面很滑。
我握著我爸爸的手。
我小心翼翼地向前移動。我覺得很緊張，而且流了很多汗。

Words

- floor 名詞 地面，地板
- slippery 形容詞 滑的
- move 動詞 移動
- forward 副詞 往前
- cautiously 副詞 小心翼翼地，謹慎地
- nervous 形容詞 緊張的
- sweat 動詞 流汗

Step 3 依樣畫葫蘆 看一下中文語意，試著使用指定的單字來完成這篇小短文。

I _____ with my family.
我和家人一起去溜冰了。

It was my _____ time* skating.
這是我第二次溜冰。

The ice floor was _____.
冰面很堅硬。

I _____ my father's hand.
我握著我爸爸的手。

I moved forward _____.
我充滿自信地向前移動。

I was _____ and sweated _____.
我覺得很興奮，而且流了一點汗。

Words

- hard 形容詞 堅硬的　副詞 努力地 　▶ confidently 副詞 充滿自信地
- excited 形容詞 感到興奮的；激動的　▶ a little 副詞 稍微，一點

Grammar Check　　time 時間；次數

time 最常見的意思是「時間」，除此之外，當想描述「已做過某件事的次數」時，也會用 time 這個字。因為次數有著如「第一次、第二次……」的順序性，所以 time 的前面必須是序數。「第一次」的英文是 first time，「最後一次」的英文則是 last time，請好好記住這些表達方式。

50

Step 4 自己動手寫寫看
請試著將想到的主題相關內容填進下方空格裡，然後寫出屬於你自己的文章。

Topic
Going _____ing

_____, _____, _____

I went _____ing _____

Learn More 單字小故事 ❷ fore（前；先前）

出現在單字開頭的 fore 具有「前」和「先前」的意思。forward 是由「前（fore）＋朝著～（ward）」所構成，因此有著「向前」的意思。forehead 是由「前（fore）＋頭（head）」所組成，因此是「額頭」的意思。那麼，foresee 又是什麼意思呢？透過構成 foresee 的「前（fore）＋看（see）」可以知道 foresee 有著「預見；預知」的意思。

Day 9 — Buying a Hat 買帽子

Step 1 認識核心動詞

need	① 需要 ② 有必要做～	need**s** 第三人稱單數現在形	need**ed** 過去形	need**ing** 現在分詞

▩ 需要

I **need** glasses because I can't see well. 我需要眼鏡，因為我看不清楚。

▩ 有必要做～：**need＋to＋動詞**

You **need to wash** your face. 你得去洗臉。

buy	① 購買 ② 買給～	buy**s** 第三人稱單數現在形	**bought** 過去形	buy**ing** 現在分詞

▩ 購買

He **bought** a new car. 他買了一台新車。

▩ 買給（某人）（某物）：**buy＋對象＋物品**

She **bought me a new coat**. 她買給了我一件新的大衣。

change	① 更換 ② 兌換	change**s** 第三人稱單數現在形	change**d** 過去形	chang**ing** 現在分詞

▩ 更換

I **changed** seats with my friend. 我和我的朋友換了座位。

▩ 兌換（錢）：**change＋錢＋into/for＋錢**

I **changed bills into coins** at the bank. 我在銀行把紙鈔兌換成了硬幣。

Tip　exchange 是「兩種物品互相交換」的意思，表示「互換」或「交流」。

Step 2 看看別人怎麼寫
請邊聽音檔邊仔細看過一遍,接著再重新唸一遍。

夏天、炎熱的
summer, hot

需要一頂帽子
need a hat

Topic
Buying a Hat

在網路上購買
buy online

今天送到
be delivered today

Saturday, July 1, Hot

As summer came, the sun became hot.

I needed a hat.

My mother bought it online two days ago.

It was delivered today.

However, I didn't like the hat so I will change it.

隨著夏天到來,太陽變得炎熱了。
我需要一頂帽子。
我媽媽兩天前在網路上買了帽子。
今天送到了。
不過,我不喜歡這頂帽子,所以我會去換貨。

Words

- **as** 連接詞 隨著～;因為～
- **become** 動詞 變成～ *過去形 became
- **online** 副詞 在網路上地
- **ago** 副詞 在(一段時間)～之前
- **deliver** 動詞 運送;投遞 *be delivered 送達,交貨

Step 3 依樣畫葫蘆 看一下中文語意，試著使用指定的單字來完成這篇小短文。

As _____ came, the _____ became _____.
隨著冬天到來，風變得寒冷了。

I _____ a _____.
我需要一條圍巾。

My mother _____ it online three days ago.
我媽媽三天前在網路上買了圍巾。

It _____* today.
今天送到了。

However, I didn't like the scarf so I will _____ it.
不過，我不喜歡這條圍巾，所以我會去換貨。

Words
- wind 名詞 風
- scarf 名詞 圍巾；披巾

Grammar Check   be delivered 送達，交貨

動詞 deliver 的意思是「運送；投遞」，be delivered 則是表達「（由某人）送達」或「完成交貨」的意思。

ex) The postman **delivers** letters. 郵差會送信。
    The TV **was delivered** to my house. 電視送到我家了。

54

Step 4　自己動手寫寫看　請試著將想到的主題相關內容填進下方空格裡，然後寫出屬於你自己的文章。

Topic
Buying _____

................., ..., ...

I need(ed) _____

_____

_____

_____

_____

Learn More　穿帽子？（wear 的語意）

以中文來說，帽子跟手套都是用「戴」這個動詞，褲子或鞋子則是用「穿」這個動詞。然而，在英文裡，無論是「戴帽子」還是「穿鞋子」，都會用具有「穿戴」之意的動詞 wear。

1. wear a hat 戴帽子
2. wear pants 穿褲子
3. wear gloves 戴手套
4. wear shoes 穿鞋子

55

Day 10　Climbing 爬山

Step 1　認識核心動詞

climb	攀登；爬上	climbs	climbed	climbing
		第三人稱單數現在形	過去形	現在分詞

▨ 攀登；爬上

He climbs the mountain every month. 他每個月都會去爬那座山。

Tip climb up 是「往上爬」的意思，climb to 則是「爬到某處」。

The monkey quickly *climbed up* the tree. 這隻猴子迅速地爬上了那棵樹。
I *climbed to* the top of the mountain. 我爬到了這座山的山頂。

grow	① 生長；發育 ② 栽培，種植	grows	grew	growing
		第三人稱單數現在形	過去形	現在分詞

▨ 生長；發育

The apple tree grew and bore fruit. 這棵蘋果樹長大結果了。

▨ 栽培，種植：**grow＋對象**

He is growing strawberries. 他正在種植草莓。

drink	喝	drinks	drank	drinking
		第三人稱單數現在形	過去形	現在分詞

▨ 喝

For your health, you should drink 8 glasses of water every day.
為了你的健康，你每天都應該喝 8 杯水。

Tip drink 可做為名詞，表示「飲料，飲品」。

Can I have a *drink*？ 可以給我一杯喝的（水或飲料）嗎？

Step 2 看看別人怎麼寫
請邊聽音檔邊仔細看過一遍，接著再重新唸一遍。

漢拏山
Mt. Halla

好天氣
good weather

Topic
Climbing

很多植物
many plants

喝涼爽的水
drink cool water

Sunday, May 22, Sunny

I climbed Mt. Halla.

The weather was good for climbing.

Many plants were growing on the mountain.

The sea view from the top was really nice.

I drank cool water at the summit.

我去爬了漢拏山。
這天氣很適合爬山。
這座山上長著很多植物。
從山頂上看到的海景真的很棒。
我在山頂喝了涼爽的水。

Words
- mountain(Mt.) 名詞 山
- weather 名詞 天氣
- plant 名詞 植物，草木
- view 名詞 視野；景色
- from 介系詞 從～（開始）
- top 名詞 頂部；山頂
- summit 名詞 山頂；頂峰

57

Step 3 依樣畫葫蘆　看一下中文語意，試著使用指定的單字來完成這篇小短文。

I _____ Mt. Halla.
我去爬了漢拏山。

The weather was _____ for climbing.
這天氣爬山很溫暖。

_____ were _____ on the mountain.
山上長著各式各樣的樹。

The _____ view from* the top was really _____.
從山頂上看到的天空景色真的很棒。

I _____ cool _____ at the summit.
我在山頂上喝了涼爽的柳橙汁。

Words

▶ warm 形容詞 溫暖的　　▶ various 形容詞 各式各樣的

Grammar Check　　from 從～（開始）

在描述「地點」時，from 意味著「出發地點」，如果描述的是「時間」，指的則是「開始的時間點」。如果要表達「抵達地點」或「結束的時間點」，則會使用 to。
ex) This restaurant is open from 3 to 7. 這間餐廳從 3 點開到 7 點。

Step 4 　自己動手寫寫看　請試著將想到的主題相關內容填進下方空格裡，然後寫出屬於你自己的文章。

Topic
Climbing

..............................., ...,

I climbed ....

....

....

....

....

Learn More　climb/go up/mount

這三個動詞都具有「向上爬」的語意，不過 climb 是「靠著自己的力量往上爬」，go up 則是「利用升降梯或纜車等運輸工具往上爬」。另一方面，「爬山」或「爬樓梯」都可以用 mount 來表達，但 mount 是比較正式的表達方式，所以不常出現在日常對話之中。

Review Test 2 (Day 6~10)

A 請根據中文正確排列英文字母並將相對應的英文動詞填入框中。

	中文	亂序	答案
1	邀請	netiiv	invite
2	來	ocem	
3	打開；開	peno	
4	遇到；碰面	teme	
5	問；詢問；要求；請求	sak	
6	（在考試中）沒有通過或不及格；失敗	laif	
7	去溜冰	og aktgnsi	
8	握著；抓住；保持	dloh	
9	需要；有必要做～	edne	
10	購買；買給	yub	
11	更換；兌換	gnahec	
12	攀登；爬上	bmlic	
13	生長；發育；栽培，種植	rwgo	
14	喝	knird	

B 請找到跟中文相對應的英文單字並標示出來，再將單字填入空格之中。

```
g t e e r t s z c t
n e r v o u s h h a
d m e c p d x n f e
e o h s r x o k z w
l u t m e g b o w s
i n a j p g i a m t
v t e v a d l q r l
e a w k r l j k f k
r i v p e m o c e b
h n j t f g g t x z
```

1 皮夾 — wallet
2 準備，籌備 — p_____
3 街道 — s_____
4 心情，情緒 — m_____
5 緊張的 — n_____
6 流汗 — s_____
7 變成～ — b_____
8 運送；投遞 — d_____
9 山 — m_____
10 天氣 — w_____

60

C 請根據中文句意將適當的字詞填入空格之中，完成英文句子。

1. They __prepared__ a present for my birthday.
   他們準備了一份生日禮物給我。

2. He said, "I _____ the _____ exam."
   他說：「我的韓國史考不及格。」

3. I moved forward _____.
   我充滿信心地向前移動。

4. As _____ came, the wind became _____.
   隨著冬天到來，風變得寒冷了。

5. The weather was _____ for climbing.
   這天氣爬山很溫暖。

D 請利用下列提示的英文來寫出符合中文句意的英文句子。

1. __I invited friends to my birthday party.__
   我邀請了朋友來我的生日派對。　　(invited / my / to / I / party / friends / birthday)

2. _____
   我在街上遇到了 Min-su。　　(Min-su / the / I / on / met / street)

3. _____
   我和家人一起去溜了冰。　　(family / went / I / my / skating / with)

4. _____
   我媽媽兩天前在網路上買了帽子。　(ago / mother / a / days / bought / My / two / hat / online)

5. _____
   這座山上長著很多植物。　　(on / Many / were / plants / the / growing / mountain)

Week 3

Day 11 **dance, sing, record** ▶ 校慶

Day 12 **borrow, forget, return** ▶ 借書

Day 13 **have, wait, take** ▶ 重感冒

Day 14 **fly, try, catch** ▶ 抓蜻蜓

Day 15 **read, love, die** ▶ 世宗大王

Review Test 3

Day 11　School Festival 校慶

Step 1　認識核心動詞

dance	① 跳舞 ② 跳（特定的舞步）	dances 第三人稱單數現在形	danced 過去形	dancing 現在分詞

▨ 跳舞

He danced to the rhythm.　他隨著節奏跳了舞。

＊在表達「隨著節奏（或旋律）跳舞」的時候，要使用 to。

▨ 跳（特定的舞步）：dance ＋ 特定的舞步

Can you dance a waltz?　你會跳華爾滋嗎？

sing	① 唱歌 ② 唱（某首歌）	sings 第三人稱單數現在形	sang 過去形	singing 現在分詞

▨ 唱歌

He sang to a piano accompaniment.　他隨著鋼琴伴奏唱了歌。

＊和 dance 一樣，在表達「隨著伴奏唱歌」時，要使用 to。

▨ 唱（某首歌）：sing ＋ 歌曲 ＋ for ＋ 對象

She sang a beautiful song for me.　她為我唱了一首好聽的歌。

record	記錄；錄製（聲音或影像等內容）	records 第三人稱單數現在形	recorded 過去形	recording 現在分詞

1 分鐘小教室

record 除了可以用來描述「用文字留下記錄」，也可以指「錄音」或「錄影」。

▨ 記錄；錄製（聲音或影像等內容）

She recorded this album in the United States.
她在美國錄製了這張專輯。

64

Step 2 看看別人怎麼寫　請邊聽音檔邊仔細看過一遍，接著再重新唸一遍。

跳舞　dance

唱歌　sing

Topic
School Festival

鼓掌　clap

看那段影片　watch the video clip

Wednesday, November 15, Cold

Today was our school festival day.

There were a lot of events. I danced to K-pop music.

Jane sang 'Let it be' by the Beatles.

Many of my friends clapped.

My friend recorded my dancing, then I watched the video clip.

今天是我們的校慶。
校慶上有很多活動。我隨著韓流音樂跳了舞。
Jane 唱了披頭四的《Let it be》。
我的很多朋友們都鼓掌了。
我朋友把我跳的舞錄了下來，後來我看了那段影片。

Words
- festival 名詞 節慶　　▶ let it be 隨它去吧，放過它吧　　▶ by 介系詞 由～（製作的，寫的）
- clap 動詞 拍手，鼓掌 名詞 鼓掌　　▶ then 副詞 之後，接著
- video clip 名詞（經過剪輯的）一段影片，一個片段

Step 3　依樣畫葫蘆　看一下中文語意，試著使用指定的單字來完成這篇小短文。

_____ was our school festival day.
昨天是我們的校慶。

There were _____ events. I _____ K-pop music.
校慶上有很多活動。我隨著韓流音樂跳了舞。

Jane _____ 'Perfect' by* Ed Sheeran.
Jane 唱了紅髮艾德的《Perfect》。

Many of my friends _____.
我的很多朋友們都歡呼了。

My friend _____ my dancing, then I _____ the video clip.
我朋友把我跳的舞錄了下來，後來我看了那段影片。

Words

▶ **yesterday** 名詞 昨天　▶ **cheer** 動詞 歡呼　名詞 歡呼，喝采

Grammar Check　**by** 在～旁邊；由～；透過～

by 最基本的意思是「在～旁邊」，所以 a house by the river 的意思是「在那條河旁邊的一間房子」，另一方面，由於待在旁邊的人勢必會對在其周圍的人事物造成直接影響，所以 by 的語意便從「在～旁邊」衍生出了「由～」和「透過～」的意思。

ex) America was discovered **by** Columbus. 美洲是由哥倫布發現的。

Step 4　**自己動手寫寫看**　請試著將想到的主題相關內容填進下方空格裡，然後寫出屬於你自己的文章。

Topic
School Festival

………………………, ………………………, ………………
Today was our school festival day.

Learn More　Ed Sheeran

Ed Sheeran（紅髮艾德）是一位英國創作歌手（singer-song writer：自己包辦作詞作曲及演唱的歌手），於 2011 年出道，在世界各地廣受歡迎。代表作品有 *Shape of You*、*Perfect*、*Bad Habits*、*Thinking Out Loud* 等等，另外，他的吉他也彈得很好。

Day 12　Borrowing Books 借書

Step 1　認識核心動詞

borrow	① 借入（物品） ② 借入（錢）	borrow**s** 第三人稱單數現在形	borrow**ed** 過去形	borrow**ing** 現在分詞

■ 借入（物品）：**borrow＋物品＋from＋對象**

　I borrowed an umbrella from Jane.　我跟 Jane 借了一把傘。

■ 借入（錢）：**borrow＋金額＋from＋對象**

　I borrowed 1 million NTD from the bank.　我跟銀行借了台幣 100 萬元。

forget	忘記；忘了	forget**s** 第三人稱單數現在形	forgot 過去形	forget**ting** 現在分詞

1 分鐘小教室

forget 用來描述「遺忘記憶中的某項人事物」。當有人說「I forgot my umbrella.」，表達的語意是「（一邊看著下雨的情境一邊說）我忘了帶傘」。如果是「弄丟物品」，則會用 lose 這個字，所以當有人說「I lost my umbrella.」，意思是「（不知道把傘放在哪裡，找不到了）我弄丟了雨傘」。

■ 忘記；忘了

　I forgot his name.　我忘了他的名字。

■ 忘了（做某件事）：**forget＋to＋動詞**

　I forgot to do my homework.
　我忘了寫作業。

return	① 歸還 ② 返回	return**s** 第三人稱單數現在形	return**ed** 過去形	return**ing** 現在分詞

■ 歸還：**return＋物品＋to＋對象**

　I returned the soccer ball to Jake.　我把那顆足球還給了 Jack。

■ （從～）返回：**return＋from＋地點（或狀態）**

　He returned from a trip yesterday.　他昨天旅行回來了。

68

Step 2　看看別人怎麼寫　請邊聽音檔邊仔細看過一遍，接著再重新唸一遍。

科學作業
science homework

圖書館
library

Topic
Borrowing Books

借期，2 個禮拜
rental period, 2 weeks

忘了還
forget to return

Tuesday, March 25, Cloudy

I needed a book to do my science homework.

I borrowed 3 books from the library.

The rental period for those books was 2 weeks.

But I forgot to return them.

I can't borrow books for a week.

我需要一本書來做我的科學作業。
我從圖書館借了 3 本書。
這些書的借期是 2 個禮拜。
但是我忘了還這些書。
我一個禮拜不能借書。

Words

▸ science 名詞 科學　▸ library 名詞 圖書館　▸ rental 名詞 租借；出租　▸ period 名詞 一段時間

Step 3 依樣畫葫蘆 看一下中文語意，試著使用指定的單字來完成這篇小短文。

I needed a book to do my _____ homework.
我需要一本書來做我的社會科作業。

I _____ 3 books from the _____.
我從這裡的圖書館借了 3 本書。

_____ for those books was 2 weeks.
這些書的借期是 2 個禮拜。

But I _____ to _____ them.
但是我忘了還這些書。

I can't borrow books for* _____.
我一個禮拜不能借書。

Words

▶ social studies 名詞 社會科　▶ local 形容詞 當地的，本地的

Grammar Check　for 達，計～（一段期間）

介系詞 for 最常用來表示某個目的，也就是「為了～」的語意。舉例來說，This is for you. 表示「這是為你（做的）」。不過 for 還能用來表達某個動作或狀態持續的「時間範圍」，也就是「達，計～（一段期間）」。如 I slept for 4 hours. 表示「我睡了 4 個小時」。除此之外，for 也能用來描述方向、原因等等，用途非常廣。

Step 4　自己動手寫寫看　請試著將想到的主題相關內容填進下方空格裡，然後寫出屬於你自己的文章。

Topic
Borrowing Books

----------, ----------,

Learn More　科目（subject）

1. science 科學
2. Korean 韓語
3. ethics 倫理與道德
4. math(mathematics) 數學
5. practical arts 工藝
6. creative experience activity 創意體驗活動

Day 13 — Bad Cold 重感冒

Step 1 認識核心動詞

have	① 得到（疾病等） ② 擁有（時間等）	has 第三人稱單數現在形	had 過去形	having 現在分詞

1 分鐘小教室

have 最基本的語意是「有」，並從基本語意衍生出了多種字義，例如，體內擁有壞菌，就是「得病」，而擁有時間則是「有時間做～」的意思。

▨ 得到（疾病等）
I have a stomachache. 我胃痛。

▨ 擁有（時間等）
I don't have time to watch TV. 我沒有時間看電視。

wait	等待	waits 第三人稱單數現在形	waited 過去形	waiting 現在分詞

▨ 等待
Please wait your turn. 請等到輪到你的時候。

▨ 等～（某人）：**wait ＋ for ＋ 對象**
Mom is waiting for me at home. 媽媽正在家裡等我。

take	① 抓 ② 吃（藥） ③ 採取（行動）	takes 第三人稱單數現在形	took 過去形	taking 現在分詞

▨ 抓
He took the rope and crossed the river. 他抓住了繩子渡河。

▨ 吃（藥）
You should take medicine three times a day. 你一天應該要吃三次藥。

▨ 採取（行動）：**take ＋（描述行動的）名詞**
I took a nap for three hours. 我小睡了三個小時。

72

Step 2 看看別人怎麼寫
請邊聽音檔邊仔細看過一遍，接著再重新唸一遍。

```
        醫院                              很多病人
      hospital                          many patients
                    ┌─────────────┐
                    │    Topic    │
                    │   Bad Cold  │
                    └─────────────┘
        等待                              吃藥
        wait                         take medicine
```

Friday, October 5, Windy

I had a bad cold. I went to the hospital.

There were many patients in the hospital.

I waited for 30 minutes.

The doctor gave me a prescription.

I took medicine and took a nap.

我得了重感冒。我去了醫院。
醫院裡有很多病人。
我等了 30 分鐘。
醫生給了我一張處方籤。
我吃了藥並小睡了一會。

Words

- **bad cold** 重感冒
- **patient** 名詞 病人　形容詞 有耐心的
- **for** 介系詞 達，計～（一段期間）
- **prescription** 名詞 處方籤
- **medicine** 名詞 藥
- **nap** 名詞 小睡；午睡

Step 3 依樣畫葫蘆　看一下中文語意，試著使用指定的單字來完成這篇小短文。

I _____ a bad cold. I went to the _____.
我得了重感冒。我去了藥局。

There were* many patients in the _____.
藥局裡有很多病人。

I _____ for 30 minutes.
我等了30分鐘。

_____ gave me medicine.
藥師給了我藥。

I _____ and took a nap.
我吃了藥並小睡了一會。

Words
- pharmacy 名詞 藥局
- pharmacist 名詞 藥師

Grammar Check　there＋be 動詞 有～

雖然 there 有著「在那裡」的意思，但其實這個句型在解讀時會忽略 there，而只讀取 be 動詞的涵義，所以這個句型的意思並非「那裡有～」，而是「有～」。如果只有一個，就用單數的 there is，如果有好幾個，那就用複數的 there are。

Step 4　自己動手寫寫看　請試著將想到的主題相關內容填進下方空格裡，然後寫出屬於你自己的文章。

Topic
_____

..................., ..., ...

I had ....

....

....

....

....

Learn More　症狀（symptom）

1. fever 發燒
2. headache 頭痛
3. runny nose 流鼻水
4. bloody nose 流鼻血
5. toothache 牙痛
6. stomachache 胃痛

Day 14 Catching Dragonflies 抓蜻蜓

Step 1 認識核心動詞

fly	① 飛 ② 飛行	flies	flew	flying
		第三人稱單數現在形	過去形	現在分詞

▨ 飛

A pigeon is flying high in the sky 一隻鴿子在天空中飛得很高。

▨ 飛行

This plane flies from Seoul to Busan. 這架飛機是從首爾飛往釜山的。

Tip fly 做為名詞時是「蒼蠅」的意思。

try	① 試圖；努力 ② 嘗試	tries	tried	trying
		第三人稱單數現在形	過去形	現在分詞

1 分鐘小教室

一般會用「try to＋動詞」來描述「努力（試圖）去實現某一件困難的事」，另一方面，「try＋V-ing」則是用來描述「嘗試去做做看一件不困難的事」。

▨ 試圖；努力：**try＋to＋動詞**

The company is trying to create a new vaccine.
那間公司正在試圖製造出新的疫苗。

▨ 嘗試：**try＋V-ing**

I tried taking this vitamin.
我嘗試過吃這款維他命。

catch	① 抓住 ② 趕上	catches	caught	catching
		第三人稱單數現在形	過去形	現在分詞

▨ 抓住

The police caught the thief. 警方抓住了小偷。

▨ 趕上：**catch up with**

I'll catch up with you soon. 我會很快趕上你。

Step 2　看看別人怎麼寫　請邊聽音檔邊仔細看過一遍，接著再重新唸一遍。

公園附近　around the park
試圖去抓住　try to catch

Topic
Catching Dragonflies

不容易的　not easy
抓到一隻　catch one

Thursday, September 12, Warm

Dragonflies were flying around the park.

I tried to catch them.

However, it was not easy.

I waited until the dragonflies sat on the leaves and stopped.

In the end, I caught one.

蜻蜓在公園附近飛來飛去。
我試圖要抓住牠們。
不過，這不是簡單的事。
我一直等到蜻蜓停在葉子上不動了的時候。
最後，我抓到了一隻。

Words

- dragonfly 名詞 蜻蜓
- around 介系詞 在～附近
- until 介系詞 直到～的時候
- leaf 名詞 葉子 *複數形 leaves
- in the end 最後，最終

Step 3 依樣畫葫蘆　看一下中文語意，試著使用指定的單字來完成這篇小短文。

_____ were _____ around the _____.
蝴蝶在花園附近飛來飛去。

I _____ them.
我試圖要抓住牠們。

However, it was _____.
然而，這很困難。

I _____ until* the _____ sat on the leaves and stopped.
我一直等到蝴蝶停在葉子上不動了的時候。

_____, I caught one.
最後，我抓到了一隻。

Words

- butterfly 名詞 蝴蝶
- garden 名詞 花園
- difficult 形容詞 困難的

Grammar Check　until 直到～的時候

句子裡的「A until B」，指的是「A 情況會一直持續到 B 情況發生為止」。The store is open until 9 p.m. 是「這間店會（中間不關店）一直開門營業到晚上 9 點的時候」，請記住這個句型所表達的「持續」語意。

Step 4 自己動手寫寫看
請試著將想到的主題相關內容填進下方空格裡，然後寫出屬於你自己的文章。

Topic
Catching _____

_____, _____, _____

Learn More 昆蟲 (insect)

1. grasshopper 蚱蜢；蝗蟲
2. beetle 甲蟲
3. cicada 蟬
4. bee 蜜蜂
5. ant 螞蟻
6. fly 蒼蠅
7. mosquito 蚊子

Day 15　King Sejong 世宗大王

Step 1　認識核心動詞

read	① 閱讀 ② 寫明；標明	read**s** 第三人稱單數現在形	read 過去形	read**ing** 現在分詞

▧ 閱讀

I read 3 books a week.　我一個禮拜會讀三本書。

▧ 寫明；標明

The sign read 'No Entry'.　那個標牌寫明了「禁止進入」。

love	① 熱愛 ② 喜歡（做～）	love**s** 第三人稱單數現在形	love**d** 過去形	lov**ing** 現在分詞

▧ 熱愛

My mom loves me so much.　我的媽媽非常愛我。

▧ 喜歡（做～）：**love＋to＋動詞**

I love to drive.　我喜歡開車。

die	死亡	die**s** 第三人稱單數現在形	die**d** 過去形	**dying** 現在分詞

▧ 死於：**die of/from＋原因**

He died of cancer last year.　他去年死於癌症。

Tip pass away（過世）是 die 的委婉表達方式。

He *passed away from* cancer last year.　他去年因癌症過世了。

Step 2　看看別人怎麼寫　請邊聽音檔邊仔細看過一遍，接著再重新唸一遍。

閱讀傳記　read a biography
朝鮮王朝　Joseon Dynasty
愛人民　love people
發明韓文字　invent Hangul

Topic: King Sejong

Saturday, February 5, Snowy

I read the biography of King Sejong.

He was the fourth king of the Joseon Dynasty.

He loved his people very much.

He found out that they could not read and write.

He invented Hangul for them. He died in 1450.

我讀了世宗大王的傳記。
他是朝鮮王朝的第四代君主。
他非常愛他的人民。
他發現人民不會讀也不會寫。
他為他們發明了韓文字。他死於西元 1450 年。

Words

- biography 名詞 傳記
- dynasty 名詞 王朝，朝代
- invent 動詞 發明
- find out 發現
- write 動詞 書寫

Step 3 依樣畫葫蘆 看一下中文語意，試著使用指定的單字來完成這篇小短文。

I _____ the biography of King Gwanggaeto.
我讀了廣開土大王的傳記。

He was the _____ king of* Goguryeo.
他是高麗王朝的第十九代君主。

He _____ his people very much.
他非常愛他的人民。

He _____ the country.
他擴張了國家。

He _____ in 412.
他死於西元 412 年。

Words

▶ expand 動詞 擴張；擴大   ▶ country 名詞 國家

Grammar Check   of ～的

of 帶有「擁有」的語意，也可以說是表達了一種「包含」的關係。這裡 the nineteenth king(A) of Goguryeo(B)，表達的是「整個高麗王朝的存在期間曾有多位君主，而廣開土大王是其中的第十九代君主」，也就是「A 包含在 B 裡（A 是 B 的一部分）」的意思。

ex) The night view of Seoul is beautiful.
　　首爾的夜景很美。（「night view(A) 夜景」包含在「Seoul(B) 首爾」裡）

Step 4　自己動手寫寫看　請試著將想到的主題相關內容填進下方空格裡，然後寫出屬於你自己的文章。

Topic
_____

_____, _____, _____

I read _____

_____

_____

_____

_____

Learn More　世界偉人

1. Thomas Edison(1847~1931) invented the phonograph.
   湯瑪士・愛迪生發明了留聲機。

2. Ludwig van Beethoven(1770~1827) was a German composer and pianist.
   貝多芬是一位德國作曲家兼鋼琴家。

3. William Shakespeare(1564-1616) was one of the greatest writers in the world.
   威廉・莎士比亞是世界上最偉大的作家之一。

Review Test 3 (Day 11~15)

A 請寫出與以下中文相對應的英文動詞。

1. 得到（疾病等）；擁有（時間等） → have
2. 飛；飛行 → f_____
3. 跳舞；跳（特定的舞步） → d_____
4. 忘記；忘了 → f_____
5. 抓；吃（藥）；採取（行動） → t_____
6. 死亡 → d_____
7. 借入（物品）；借入（錢） → b_____
8. 等待 → w_____
9. 試圖；努力；嘗試 → t_____
10. 唱歌；唱（某首歌） → s_____
11. 歸還；返回 → r_____
12. 記錄；錄製（聲音或影像等） → r_____
13. 抓住；趕上 → c_____
14. 熱愛；喜歡（做～） → l_____
15. 閱讀；寫明；標明 → r_____

B 請將英文單字與相對應的中文字義連起來。

1. patient   ⓐ 圖書館
2. clap   ⓑ 病人；有耐心的
3. leaf   ⓒ 蜻蜓
4. library   ⓓ 拍手，鼓掌
5. dragonfly   ⓔ 葉子
6. festival   ⓕ 發明
7. invent   ⓖ 節慶
8. medicine   ⓗ 科學
9. write   ⓘ 書寫
10. science   ⓙ 藥

C 請根據中文句意將適當的字詞填入空格之中，完成英文句子。

1. There were __a lot of__ events.
   有很多活動。

2. _____ for 3 books was 2 weeks.
   三本書的借期是 2 個禮拜。

3. _____ gave me medicine.
   藥師給了我藥。

4. _____, I caught one.
   最後，我抓到了一隻。

5. He _____ the country.
   他擴張了國家。

D 請利用下列提示的英文動詞來寫出符合中文句意的英文句子。

1. dance — I danced to K-pop music.
   我隨著韓流音樂跳了舞。

2. borrow _____
   我從圖書館借了 3 本書。

3. wait _____
   我等了 30 分鐘。

4. try, catch _____
   我試圖要抓住蜻蜓。

5. love _____
   他非常愛他的人民。

Week 4

Day 16 **help, send** ▸ 傳訊息

Day 17 **think, sell** ▸ 跳蚤市場

Day 18 **exercise, start, walk** ▸ 運動

Day 19 **become, discuss, agree**
　　　▸ 討論國中入學的事

Day 20 **learn, practice, believe**
　　　▸ 學吉他

Review Test 4

Day 16 Sending a Message 傳訊息

Step 1 認識核心動詞

help	① 幫助 ② 取用（食物等）	**help**s 第三人稱單數現在形	**help**ed 過去形	**help**ing 現在分詞

■ 幫助：**help**＋對象

Can you help me? 你可以幫我嗎？

■ 幫助：**help**＋對象＋**with**＋對象須做的事

I helped her with her housework. 我幫助她做（她的）家事。

■ 幫（某人）做（某事）：**help**＋對象＋**(to)**＋動詞

He helped me wash the car. 他幫我洗了車。

＊一般 to 會被省略。

■ 取用（食物等）

Help yourself. 別客氣，自己來（請自行取用）。

＊一般來說，會用 eat 來說「吃東西」，但當想對客人表示「可以自己去拿想吃的，盡情享用、不用客氣」時，會說 Help yourself。

Tip help 也可做為名詞，表示「幫助」或「有幫助的人或東西」。

send	發送；寄送； 傳送	**send**s 第三人稱單數現在形	**sent** 過去形	**send**ing 現在分詞

■ （將～）發送；寄送；傳送給～：**send**＋物品／電子郵件／訊息＋**to**＋對象

I sent a package to my aunt. 我寄了一個包裹給我的阿姨。

■ （將～）發送；寄送；傳送給～：**send**＋對象＋物品／電子郵件／訊息

She sent me an email. 她寄給了我一封電子郵件。

Tip （從～）收到；得到：receive＋物品／電子郵件／訊息＋from＋對象

I received a letter from my grandmother.
我從我奶奶那裡收到了一封信。

88

Step 2 看看別人怎麼寫　請邊聽音檔邊仔細看過一遍，接著再重新唸一遍。

Topic: Sending a Message

- 不擅長數學　not good at math
- John 幫助我　John helps me
- 傳給 John 一條訊息　send John a message
- John 回覆　John sends a reply

Wednesday, May 8, Clear

I'm not good at math.

I asked John for help.

John helped me solve a math problem.

I sent him a message in the evening, "Thank you for helping me."

An hour later, John sent a reply, "I was glad to help you."

我不擅長數學。
我請 John 幫忙。
John 幫我解決了一題數學。
我在晚上傳了一條訊息給他，說：「謝謝你幫我。」
在一個小時後，他回覆說：「我很高興能幫你。」

Words

- be good at 擅長～
- ask for help （向～）求助
- solve 動詞 解決；解答（問題等）
- problem 名詞 問題
- in the evening 在晚上
- later 副詞 後來；以後
- reply 名詞 回覆，答覆　動詞 回覆

Step 3 依樣畫葫蘆 看一下中文語意，試著使用指定的單字來完成這篇小短文。

I'm not _____.
我不擅長英文。

I _____ Sharon for help.
我請 Sharon 幫忙。

Sharon _____ me _____.
Sharon 幫我寫了英文。

I _____ her a message _____, "Thank you for* helping me."
我在晚上傳了一條訊息給她，說：「謝謝妳幫我。」

Sharon sent a _____ soon, "I was _____ to help you."
她很快回覆說：「我很高興能幫你。」

Words

▶ write 動詞 書寫　▶ night 名詞 夜晚　▶ soon 副詞 很快，不久　▶ glad 形容詞 高興的；樂意的

Grammar Check　Thank you for~ 感謝你～

因為 for 的後面必須接名詞，所以若想接具動詞意義的表達方式時，必須將該動詞名詞化（變成 V-ing）才行。請把一些常用的表達方式記下來，未來會非常有用。

1 Thank you for your time. 感謝您抽出時間。
2 Thank you for listening.（對聽眾）感謝您的聆聽。
3 Thank you for coming. 感謝您的到來。
4 Thank you for joining us. 感謝您加入我們。

Step 4　自己動手寫寫看　請試著將想到的主題相關內容填進下方空格裡，然後寫出屬於你自己的文章。

Topic
Sending a Message

Learn More　單字小故事 ❸ re（返回；再次）

字首 re 具有「返回」的意思，具體想要表達的語意，就像是在賣場排隊結完帳後，「返回」到隊伍後方「再次」購物一樣，因此字首 re 也有「再次」之意。reply 是「再次（re）＋折疊（ply）」，表示「打開摺疊的信紙，寫完回信後再次摺起來」，故字義是「答覆，回覆」。return 的組成是「再次（re）＋轉（向）（turn）」，表示「返回」的意思。rehearsal 則是由「再次（re）＋重複，原字義是「耙」（hear）＋名詞字尾（sal）」構成，字義是「（表演等的）排練」。

Day 17 Flea Market 跳蚤市場

Step 1 認識核心動詞

think	思考；認為；想	thinks	thought	thinking
		第三人稱單數現在形	過去形	現在分詞

▨ 思考；想（關於～的事）：**think＋about＋主題**

I'll think about it later. 我晚點會想想這件事。

▨ 認為（是～）：**think＋(that)＋主詞＋動詞**

Do you think (that) he is 10 years old? 你認為他是 10 歲嗎？
I thought he was kind. 我以為他很善良。

sell	① 賣 ② 售出	sells	sold	selling
		第三人稱單數現在形	過去形	現在分詞

▨ 賣

The supermarket sells meat at a discount.
這間超市以折扣價販售肉品。
* at a discount 以折扣價

▨ （以某金額）賣（物品）給（對象）：**sell＋物品＋to＋對象（for＋金額）**

I sold my car to my friend for 1 million NTD.
我用台幣 100 萬元的價格把我的車賣給了我朋友。

▨ 售出

This book sold 10,000 copies in one month.
這本書在一個月內售出了 10,000 本。

> **Tip** 購買（物品）：buy　* 過去形是 bought
> I bought a new bag. 我買了一個新包包。

Step 2　看看別人怎麼寫　請邊聽音檔邊仔細看過一遍，接著再重新唸一遍。

在學校　　　　　　　　　　　　　　　　　　要帶什麼
at school　　　　　　　　　　　　　　　　　what to take

Topic
Flea Market

玩具　　　　　　　　　　　　　　　　　　　賣掉其中一些
toys　　　　　　　　　　　　　　　　　　　sell some of them

Tuesday, October 5, Cool

There will be a flea market at school tomorrow.

I *thought about* what to take.

There are a lot of toys in my room.

I will *sell* some of them tomorrow.

I'm looking forward to tomorrow.

明天在學校會有跳蚤市場。
我想了想要帶什麼。
我的房間裡有很多玩具。
明天我會賣掉其中一些。
我很期待明天。

Words

- flea 名詞 跳蚤　　- flea market 跳蚤市場　　- take 動詞 帶去，拿去　　- a lot of 很多
- some of 其中一些～　　- look forward to 期待～

Step 3 依樣畫葫蘆　看一下中文語意，試著使用指定的單字來完成這篇小短文。

There will be a flea market _____ tomorrow.
明天公寓社區裡會有跳蚤市場。

I _____ what to take.*
我想了想要帶什麼。

There are a lot of _____ in my room.
我的房間裡有很多洋娃娃。

I will _____ some of them tomorrow.
明天我會賣掉其中一些。

I'm _____ tomorrow.
我很期待明天。

Words

▸ **apartment** 名詞 公寓　▸ **complex** 名詞 複合體；綜合設施　形容詞 複合的；複雜的

Grammar Check　　what to＋動詞 該做什麼

慣用表達「what to＋動詞」大多出現在 know（知道）、think（思考）、tell（說）等動詞的後方，what to eat 表示「吃什麼」，what to sell 則表示「賣什麼」。那麼，know what to eat 又是什麼意思呢？其實就是「知道該吃什麼」的意思。

Step 4 自己動手寫寫看　請試著將想到的主題相關內容填進下方空格裡，然後寫出屬於你自己的文章。

Topic
Flea Market

..................., ..., ...

There will be a flea market ....

Learn More　表示「數量眾多」的常用表達方式

1. a lot of ＋可數／不可數名詞　ex) a lot of cars (○), a lot of water (○)
2. many ＋可數名詞　ex) many books (○), many information (✗)
3. much ＋不可數名詞　ex) much books (✗), much information (○)

Day 18 Exercise 運動

Step 1 認識核心動詞

exercise	① 運動 ② 鍛鍊；操練	exercises 第三人稱單數現在形	exercised 過去形	exercising 現在分詞

◼ 運動
I am tired because I **exercised** a lot yesterday. 我很累，因為我昨天運動量很大。

◼ 鍛鍊；操練
She **exercises** her dog every day. 她每天都會訓練她的狗。

> **Tip** exercise 也可做為名詞，除了「運動」之外，也是「練習題」的意思。在學校寫的「習題」就可以用 exercise 這個單字來表達。

start	① 開始，著手 ② 開始 ③ 出發	starts 第三人稱單數現在形	started 過去形	starting 現在分詞

◼ 開始，著手：start＋對象／start＋V-ing
He **starts** work at eight. 他在八點開始工作。
He **started doing** his homework. 他開始做他的回家作業了。

◼ 開始
The performance **starts** at 9 o'clock. 那場表演在九點鐘開始。

◼ 出發
The bus **starts** on time. 那輛巴士準時發車。

walk	行走	walks 第三人稱單數現在形	walked 過去形	walking 現在分詞

◼ 行走
My dad **walks** 30 minutes every day. 我爸爸每天會走路 30 分鐘。

> **Tip** walk 做為名詞時是「走路」或「散步」的意思，go for a walk 表示「去散步」。

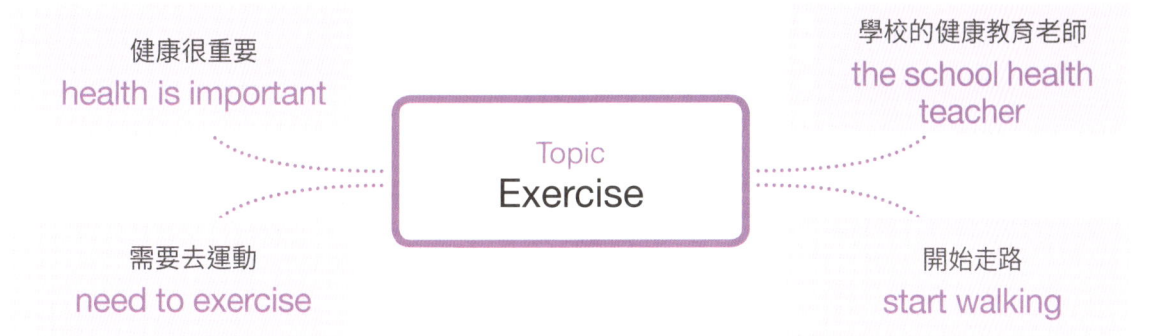

Step 2　看看別人怎麼寫　請邊聽音檔邊仔細看過一遍，接著再重新唸一遍。

健康很重要
health is important

學校的健康教育老師
the school health teacher

Topic
Exercise

需要去運動
need to exercise

開始走路
start walking

Thursday, June 3, Warm

Many people say health is the most important thing.

Today, the school health teacher said, "We should **exercise** three days a week."

I don't like exercising; I like playing games.

I need to exercise for my health.

I will **start walking** every day from tomorrow.

　　　　　　　　　有很多人都說健康是最重要的事。
　　　　　學校的健康教育老師今天說：「我們應該每週運動三天。」
　　　　　　　　　　　我不喜歡運動；我喜歡玩遊戲。
　　　　　　　　　　我需要為了我的健康去運動。
　　　　　　　　　　我從明天開始會每天去走路。

Words
- most 副詞 最；最大程度地
- important 形容詞 重要的
- health teacher 健康教育老師
- should＋動詞 應該做～
- a 冠詞 每～（＝per）

Step 3 依樣畫葫蘆　看一下中文語意，試著使用指定的單字來完成這篇小短文。

_____ say health is the most* _____.
大人都說健康是最重要的事。

Today, the school health teacher said, "We _____ three days a week."
今天學校的健康教育老師說：「我們應該每週運動三天。」

I don't like exercising; I like _____.
我不喜歡運動；我喜歡看電視。

I _____ for my health.
我需要為了我的健康去運動。

I will _____ every _____ from tomorrow.
我從明天開始會兩天去走一次路。

Words

- **adult** 名詞 大人，成年人
- **every other day** 每隔一天，兩天一次

Grammar Check　the most 最～的

the most 是指「眾多之中最～」，而「the most＋形容詞＋名詞」表達的是「最～的（名詞）」的意思。舉例來說，the most important event 的意思便是「最重要的活動」，請記得這裡使用的形容詞，必須有 3 個以上的音節。

Step 4 自己動手寫寫看
請試著將想到的主題相關內容填進下方空格裡，然後寫出屬於你自己的文章。

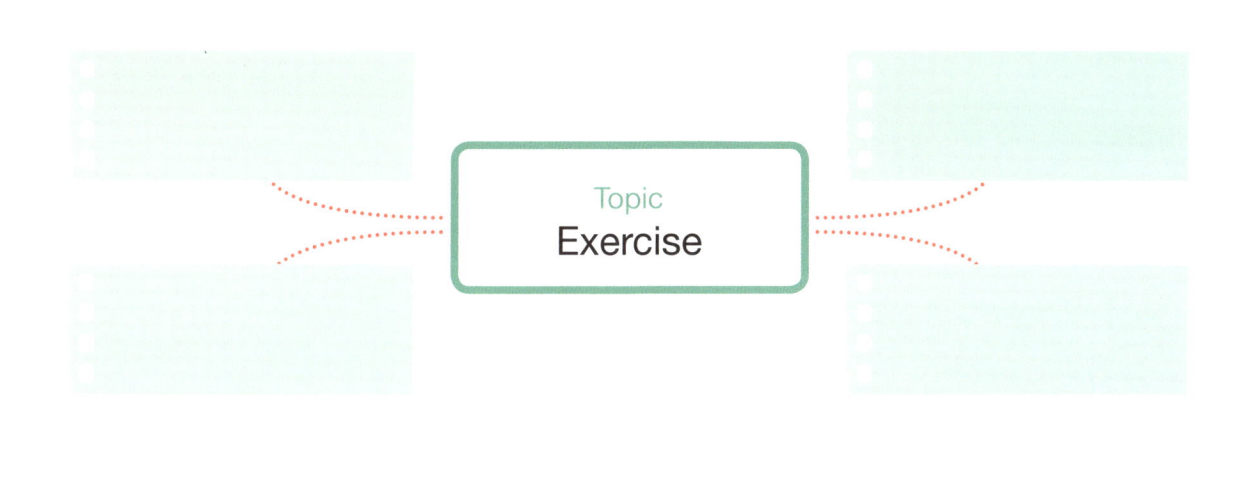

Topic
Exercise

..................., ..., ...

Many people say ....

....

....

....

Learn More — work out

exercise 跟 work out 都常被用來表示「運動」的意思，但兩者的語意略有差異。exercise 指的是走路、跑跳、體操等的一般運動，work out 則大多用來表示為了增肌而做的健身運動。

ex) Running is a good exercise. 跑步是一項很好的運動。
　　 I work out at the gym. 我會在健身房健身。

Day 19 Discussing Middle School Entrance 討論國中入學的事

> Step 1 認識核心動詞

become	成為～	becomes 第三人稱單數現在形	became 過去形	becoming 現在分詞

▨ 成為～

He **became** a famous singer. 他成為了一位有名的歌手。

Tip 上面例句中的主詞（He）跟補語（a famous singer）指的是同一個人。這是 become 這個動詞的特色，請牢記在心。

discuss	討論（關於～）	discusses 第三人稱單數現在形	discussed 過去形	discussing 現在分詞

1分鐘小教室

discuss 這個單字本身就帶有「關於」之意，所以不能與表示「關於」的 about 一起出現。
She discussed about her plans with her friend.（X）

▨ （和～）討論（關於～）：**discuss＋主題＋with＋對象**

She **discussed** her plans **with** her friend.
她和她的朋友討論了（關於）她的計畫（的事）。

agree	① 同意～ ② 達成共識	agrees 第三人稱單數現在形	agreed 過去形	agreeing 現在分詞

▨ 同意～：**agree with＋主題／agree with＋對象（about＋主題）**

The teacher **agreed with** my opinion. 老師同意我的意見。

▨ 達成共識：**agree＋about＋主題／agree＋to＋動詞**

We **agreed to eat** hamburgers. 我們達成共識要去吃漢堡。

100

Step 2 看看別人怎麼寫 請邊聽音檔邊仔細看過一遍，接著再重新唸一遍。

國中生
middle school student

和朋友同一個學校
the same school as my friend

Topic
Discussing Middle School Entrance

討論國中入學的事
discuss middle school entrance

附近的學校
a nearby school

Sunday, November 12, Cold

I will **become** a middle school student next year.

I **discussed** middle school entrance **with** my mom.

I wanted to go to the same school as my friend.

However, she wanted me to go to a nearby school.

I talked to her for one hour, and she **agreed with** my idea.

我明年要成為國中生了。
我和我媽媽討論了國中入學的事。
我想和我的朋友去上同一個學校。
不過，她想要我去上附近的學校。
我和她談了一個小時，然後她同意了我的想法。

Words

▸ middle 形容詞 中間的 名詞 中央　▸ entrance 名詞 入學；進入
▸ the same A as B 和 B 一樣的 A　▸ nearby 形容詞 附近的，近處的

Step 3 依樣畫葫蘆 看一下中文語意，試著使用指定的單字來完成這篇小短文。

I will _____ a middle school student next year.
我明年要成為國中生了。

I _____ middle school entrance _____ my mom.
我和我媽媽討論了國中入學的事。

I wanted to go to an _____.
我想去上藝術中學。

However,* she wanted me to go to a _____.
不過，她想要我去上附近的學校。

I talked to her for one hour, and she _____.
我和她談了一個小時，然後她同意了我的決定。

Words

▸ art 名詞 藝術   ▸ decision 名詞 決定

Grammar Check   however vs. but 不過，但是

雖然 however 跟 but 都是「不過」和「但是」的意思，但兩者的詞性卻不同。however 是副詞，而 but 是連接詞。連接詞的功能是「連接」句子，所以 but 的後面可以直接接上句子。另一方面，副詞的功能則是用來「修飾」句子，所以 however 的後面會加上逗號（,），將用來修飾整個句子的 however 和後面所接的句子分隔開來。

ex) I was hungry but I didn't eat.　我很餓，但我沒有吃。
　　I was hungry. However, I didn't eat.　我很餓。不過，我沒有吃。

Step 4　**自己動手寫寫看**　請試著將想到的主題相關內容填進下方空格裡，然後寫出屬於你自己的文章。

Topic
Discussing _____

_____, _____, _____

Learn More　學校

1. kindergarten, preschool 幼稚園
2. elementary school 國小
3. middle school 國中
4. high school 高中
5. university 綜合性大學 *校內系所多元，通常會由多個分科學院聯合組成的綜合性大學。
6. college 大專，學院 *集中研究某一領域的大專院校。

103

Day 20　Learning Guitar 學吉他

Step 1　認識核心動詞

learn	學；學習	learn**s** 第三人稱單數現在形	learn**ed** 過去形	learn**ing** 現在分詞

▨ 學
　I **learn** English at school.　我在學校學英文。

▨ 學習（做某件事）：**learn＋to＋動詞**
　I will **learn to swim** during vacation.　我在放假期間會去學游泳。
　Tip study 指的是「積極努力鑽研」，learn 則是「向別人學習並讓自己熟練」的一整個學習過程。

practice	練習	practice**s** 第三人稱單數現在形	practice**d** 過去形	practic**ing** 現在分詞

▨ 練習：**practice＋項目／practice＋V-ing**
　He **practiced writing** every day.　他以前每天練習寫作。
　Tip practice 當名詞時，除了「練習」，也有「慣例」或「常規」的意思。

believe	相信；認為～	believe**s** 第三人稱單數現在形	believe**d** 過去形	believ**ing** 現在分詞

▨ 相信
　I don't **believe** you.　我不相信你。

▨ 認為～：**believe＋(that)＋主詞＋動詞**
　The police **believe (that) he is** the criminal.　警方認為他是那名歹徒。
　＊ the police＋複數動詞

▨ 相信（某種存在或人）：**believe in**
　Do you **believe in** God?　你相信有神嗎？

104

Step 2 看看別人怎麼寫
請邊聽音檔邊仔細看過一遍，接著再重新唸一遍。

我的哥哥
my older brother

彈吉他
play the guitar

Topic
Learning Guitar

練習
practice

相信我自己
believe in myself

Wednesday, August 11, Hot

My older brother is good at playing the guitar.

I learned to play the guitar from him.

My hands hurt when I played the guitar.

However, I feel better when I play the guitar.

I will practice the guitar every day. I believe in myself.

我的哥哥很會彈吉他。
我從他那裡學了彈吉他。
我彈吉他時手會痛。
不過，我在彈吉他時心情會比較好。
我會每天練習彈吉他。我相信我自己。

Words

- older 形容詞 較年長的
- hurt 動詞 疼痛 *過去形 hurt
- better 形容詞 更好的，較好的
- myself 代名詞 我自己

Step 3 依樣畫葫蘆　看一下中文語意，試著使用指定的單字來完成這篇小短文。

My older* _____ is _____ playing the _____.
我的姐姐很擅長彈鋼琴。

I _____ play the piano from her.
我從她那裡學了彈鋼琴。

_____ hurt when I played the piano.
我在彈鋼琴時手臂會痛。

However, I _____ when I play the piano.
不過，我在彈鋼琴時心情會比較好。

I will _____ the piano every day. I _____ in myself.
我會每天練習彈鋼琴。我相信我自己。

Words
▸ arm 名詞 手臂

Grammar Check　比較級 er，表示「更～的」

在形容詞的字尾加上 er，就可以用來表示「更～的」的意思。在「old（年老的）」的字尾加上 er，就是「更年老的，年紀更大的」，smart（聰明的）加上 er，則是「更聰明的」。

* 形成比較級的方法
1. 字尾是 e 的形容詞：+r　ex) large → larger 更大的
2. 字尾是「單母音＋單子音」的形容詞：重複最後一個子音再+er　ex) big → bigger 更大的
3. 字尾是「子音＋y」的形容詞：將 y 替換成 i 再+er　ex) happy → happier 更快樂的

Step 4 自己動手寫寫看
請試著將想到的主題相關內容填進下方空格裡，然後寫出屬於你自己的文章。

Topic
Learning _____

Learn More　跟「練習」有關的英文俗語／名言

1. **Practice makes perfect.** 熟能生巧。
   *perfect 形容詞 完美的
2. **Patience and diligence, like faith, remove mountains.**
   耐心與勤勞如同信念，能夠移山。
   *patience 名詞 耐心　diligence 名詞 勤勞　faith 名詞 信念；信任　remove 動詞 移除

Review Test 4 (Day 16~20)

A 請根據中文正確排列英文字母並將相對應的英文動詞填入框中。

#	中文	字母	答案
1	賣；售出	lles	sell
2	成為～	cmoeeb	
3	行走	kalw	
4	學；學習	nreal	
5	幫助；取用（食物等）	eplh	
6	相信	veebiel	
7	同意～；達成共識	geaer	
8	運動；鍛鍊；操練	ereescix	
9	發送；寄送；傳送	dnes	
10	開始；著手；出發	sratt	
11	討論（關於～）	ssidsuc	
12	思考；認為；想	kniht	
13	練習	ariteccp	

B 請找到跟中文相對應的英文單字並標示出來，再將單字填入空格之中。

```
e s t u e b n p t f
n o c d f e r h n l
t l a q a o d i e e
r v f r b l k p m s
a e b l u w n x t y
n y e o n b r z r m
c m h f n k p s a p
e s r e t t e b p j
e a e l f a i m a v
i m p o r t a n t d
```

#	中文	答案
1	解決；解答（問題等）	solve
2	問題	p_____
3	跳蚤	f_____
4	公寓	a_____
5	應該做～	s_____
6	重要的	i_____
7	入學；進入	e_____
8	附近的；近處的	n_____
9	更好的，較好的	b_____
10	我自己	m_____

108

C 請根據中文句意將適當的字詞填入空格之中，完成英文句子。

1. I'm not ___good at English___.
   我不擅長英文。

2. I'm _____ tomorrow.
   我很期待明天。

3. _____ say health is the most _____.
   大人都說健康是最重要的事。

4. I wanted to go to an _____ _____.
   我想去上藝術中學。

5. _____ hurt when I played the piano.
   我在彈鋼琴時手臂會痛。

D 請利用下列提示的英文來寫出符合中文句意的英文句子。

1. ___John helped me solve a math problem.___
   John 幫我解決了數學題。 (John / math / helped / solve / me / problem / a)

2. _____
   我想了想該帶什麼去。 (I / take / about / thought / to / what)

3. _____
   我會從明天開始每天去走路。 (tomorrow / I / from / will / start / day / walking / every)

4. _____
   我和我媽媽討論了國中入學的事。 (my / I / school / middle / with / discussed / entrance / mom)

5. _____
   我會每天練習彈吉他。 (day / the / I / practice / every / guitar / will)

109

Week 5

Day 21 **feel, call, talk** ▶ 無聊的日子

Day 22 **collect, listen, turn** ▶ 我的嗜好

Day 23 **paint, take, stay** ▶ 壞掉的腳踏車

Day 24 **congratulate, give, thank** ▶ 恭喜！

Day 25 **decide, eat, drive** ▶ 去外面吃

Review Test 5

Day 21 Boring Day 無聊的日子

Step 1 認識核心動詞

feel	① 感受（情緒等） ② （透過觸摸來）感受	feels	felt	feeling
		第三人稱單數現在形	過去形	現在分詞

▧ 感受（情緒等）

I **felt good** because I got 100 points in math.
我覺得很棒（心情很好），因為我的數學拿了 100 分。

▧ （透過觸摸來）感受

I **felt the warmth** of my mother's hands. 我感受到了母親手掌的暖意。

call	① 呼叫，喊叫 ② 打電話	calls	called	calling
		第三人稱單數現在形	過去形	現在分詞

▧ 呼叫，喊叫

I **called** him loudly 我大聲叫他。

▧ 叫（A 成 B）：**call＋A＋B** ＊也可以表達「將 A 命名為 B」的意思。

People **call him Peter Pan**. 人們叫他彼得潘。

▧ 打電話

I will **call** you back later. 我晚點會回你電話。

talk	說話；談論	talks	talked	talking
		第三人稱單數現在形	過去形	現在分詞

1 分鐘小教室

to 表達的是「方向」，所以 talk to 表示「對～說話」，with 是「和～」的意思，所以 talk with 表示「和～談論」。

▧ （對～）說話：**talk＋to＋對象（about＋主題）**

I **talked to my friend** about the sports day.
我對我朋友說了有關運動會的事。

▧ （和～）談論：**talk＋with＋對象（about＋主題）**

I **talked with my friend** about the sports day.
我和我朋友談論了有關運動會的事。

Step 2 看看別人怎麼寫 請邊聽音檔邊仔細看過一遍,接著再重新唸一遍。

覺得無聊
feel bored

沒有接電話
don't answer the phone

Topic
Boring Day

媽媽很忙
mom is busy

看書
read books

Sunday, February 20, Snowy

I *felt* bored all day.

I *called* my friend but he didn't answer the phone.

I tried *talking to* my mom.

However, she was busy with housework.

In the end, I spent my time reading books.

我一整天都覺得很無聊。
我打給了我的朋友,但他沒接電話。
我試著去和我媽媽說話。
但是她忙著做家事。
最後,我把時間拿來看書了。

Words
- bored 形容詞 覺得無聊的
- answer 動詞 回應;答覆
- try＋V-ing 試著~
- housework 名詞 家事
- spend 動詞 花費(時間);花(錢) *過去形 spent

Step 3 依樣畫葫蘆　看一下中文語意，試著使用指定的單字來完成這篇小短文。

I _____ all day.
我一整天都覺得很無聊。

I _____ Kevin but he _____ to talk with me.
我打給了 Kevin，但他沒時間跟我聊天。

I _____ to my _____.
我試著去和我弟弟說話。

However, he was busy with _____.
但是他忙著做回家功課。

In the end, I spent* my time _____.
最後，我把時間拿來整理我的房間了。

Words

▸ have time 有時間　▸ tidy up 整理；收拾

Grammar Check　spend＋時間／金錢＋V-ing　花費時間／金錢做～

spend 後面接時間的話，表示「花了多少時間」，此時後面若再接上「V-ing」，則表示「花了多少時間做～」。spend 後面接金錢的話，表示「花了多少錢」，後方接上的「V-ing」，則表示「花了多少錢做～」。

ex) I spent a week studying math.（時間）　我花了一個禮拜念數學。
　　I spent a million won traveling.（金錢）　我花 100 萬韓元旅行。

Step 4　自己動手寫寫看　請試著將想到的主題相關內容填進下方空格裡，然後寫出屬於你自己的文章。

Topic
Boring Day

..................., ...,

I felt bored all day.

Learn More　「電話」相關的表達方式

1. This is ＋名字. （接電話的人）我是 ．
2. (May I ask) who is calling?（不好意思，請問）哪裡找呢？
3. What is this about? 有什麼事呢？
4. Please feel free to call me. 請隨時跟我聯絡。
5. Could you speak up? 可以請你大聲一點嗎？

115

Day 22　My hobby 我的嗜好

Step 1　認識核心動詞

collect	收集；使集合	collect**s**	collect**ed**	collect**ing**
		第三人稱單數現在形	過去形	現在分詞

■ 收集；使集合

We can **collect** a lot of information from the Internet.
我們可以從網路上收集到很多資訊。
She **collects** stamps.　她有在集郵。

listen	① 聆聽 ② 聽從	listen**s**	listen**ed**	listen**ing**
		第三人稱單數現在形	過去形	現在分詞

1 分鐘小教室

listen 跟 hear 都具有「聽」的語意，但 listen 所表達的是「有意識地專心聆聽」，例如聽力測驗或聆聽音樂等的情境，而 hear 描述的則是透過聽覺「無意識地聽到聲音」，例如聽到雷聲或海浪聲等。

■ 聆聽：**listen＋to＋對象（聲音）**

I often **listen to** pop songs.
我常常聽流行歌。

■ 聽從：**listen＋to＋忠告（或要求）**

You should **listen to** your teacher's advice.
你應該聽從你們老師的建議。

turn	① 轉向 ② 使轉動	turn**s**	turn**ed**	turn**ing**
		第三人稱單數現在形	過去形	現在分詞

■ 轉向

Go straight 2 blocks and **turn** right at the corner. 直走兩個街區，然後在轉角處右轉。

■ 使轉動

He **turned** the steering wheel to go home. 他轉動了方向盤要回家。

Tip turn on 是「打開（廣播、電視、電燈等）」的意思。

116

Step 2 看看別人怎麼寫 請邊聽音檔邊仔細看過一遍，接著再重新唸一遍。

收集專輯
collect albums

聽專輯裡的音樂
listen to album music

Topic
My Hobby

打開智慧型電視
turn on the smart TV

看 MV（音樂錄影帶）
watch music videos

Friday, May 12, Warm

My hobby is collecting my favorite singer's albums.

I have over twenty albums.

I listen to album music whenever I have time.

I sometimes turn on the smart TV and watch music videos.

I try easy dances while watching the music video.

我的嗜好是收集我最喜歡的歌手的專輯。
我擁有超過二十張專輯。
我一有時間就會聽專輯裡的音樂。
我偶爾會打開智慧型電視看 MV（音樂錄影帶）。
我在看 MV（音樂錄影帶）時會一邊試著跳簡單的舞步。

Words

- hobby 名詞 嗜好，興趣
- favorite 形容詞 最喜歡的
- whenever 連接詞 每當～
- sometimes 副詞 偶爾，有時

Step 3 依樣畫葫蘆　看一下中文語意，試著使用指定的單字來完成這篇小短文。

My hobby is _____ my favorite singer's albums.
我的嗜好是收集我最喜歡的歌手的專輯。

I have over _____ albums.
我擁有超過三十張專輯。

I _____ album music _____.
我幾乎每天都會聽專輯裡的音樂。

I sometimes _____* the smart TV and _____ music videos.
我偶爾會打開智慧型電視看 MV（音樂錄影帶）。

I _____ easy dances _____ watching the music video.
我在看 MV（音樂錄影帶）時會一邊試著跳簡單的舞步。

Words

▶ thirty 形容詞 三十　▶ almost 副詞 幾乎，大部分

Grammar Check　　turn on 打開～

基本字義是「轉向；使轉動」的 turn，搭配我們在 Day 7 時學過的「on 具有『接觸』之意」，組成了片語 turn on。當轉動（turn）兩條電線並讓電線互相接觸（on）時，就會產生電流，因此表達的是「打開～」的語意。另一方面，off 是 on 的反義詞，具有「分離」之意，所以 turn off 指的即是「轉動兩條電線讓兩者分離」，因此表達的是「關掉～」的意思。

Step 4　自己動手寫寫看

請試著將想到的主題相關內容填進下方空格裡，然後寫出屬於你自己的文章。

Topic
My Hobby

_____, _____, _____

My hobby is _____

_____

_____

_____

_____

Learn More　數字表達

10	ten	60	sixty
20	twenty	70	seventy
30	thirty	80	eighty
40	forty	90	ninety
50	fifty	100	hundred

Day 23　Broken Bike 壞掉的腳踏車

Step 1　認識核心動詞

paint	油漆；塗上顏色	paint**s** 第三人稱單數現在形	paint**ed** 過去形	paint**ing** 現在分詞

▨ 油漆；塗上顏色：**paint＋對象（顏色）**

He **painted the door** green.
他將那扇門漆成了綠色。

take	① 搭乘（交通工具） ② 花費（時間等）	take**s** 第三人稱單數現在形	took 過去形	tak**ing** 現在分詞

1 分鐘小教室

正如在 Day 13 中所提到的，take 最基本的字義是「抓」。從「抓住（路過的計程車或火車等）」的意象，衍生出「搭乘（交通工具）」之意。搭乘交通工具移動時，時間也會隨之流逝，因此也衍生出了「花費（時間等）」的意思。

▨ 搭乘（交通工具）

He **takes** a taxi to work every day.
他每天都搭計程車去上班。

▨ 花費（時間等）

It **took** 2 hours to do my homework.
做回家功課花了我兩個小時。

stay	暫留；停留	stay**s** 第三人稱單數現在形	stay**ed** 過去形	stay**ing** 現在分詞

▨ 暫留；停留：**stay＋in/at**

He will **stay in** Seoul for 2 weeks.　他會在首爾待兩個禮拜。

Tip stay 後面加上 up，意思是「停留在清醒的狀態」，也就是「熬夜」的意思。
　　I *stayed up* all night. 我整晚沒睡。

Step 2 看看別人怎麼寫
請邊聽音檔邊仔細看過一遍，接著再重新唸一遍。

壞掉
break

修好和上漆
fix and paint

Topic
Broken Bike

花 2 個小時
takes 2 hours

待在家裡
stay at home

Saturday, October 2, Foggy

I hit a tree while riding my bike, and it broke.

My dad fixed and *painted* my bike today.

I helped him paint.

It *took* 2 hours to finish the work.

After all, I *stayed at* home and helped my dad all afternoon.

我在騎腳踏車的時候撞到了樹，結果腳踏車就壞了。
我爸今天幫我把腳踏車修好和上漆。
我幫著他上了漆。
這件事花了兩個小時才完成。
結果，我整個下午都待在家裡幫忙我爸了。

Words
- ride 動詞 騎乘（腳踏車或馬等） ▸ bike 名詞 腳踏車；機車 ▸ fix 動詞 修理；使固定
- finish 動詞 完成；結束 ▸ after all 結果，最後

121

Step 3 依樣畫葫蘆　看一下中文語意，試著使用指定的單字來完成這篇小短文。

I hit the wall while _____, and it _____.
我在搬書架的時候撞到了牆，結果書架就壞了。

My dad fixed and _____ my _____ today.
我爸今天把我的書架修好並上漆

I helped him _____.
我幫著他上了漆。

It _____ * 2 hours to _____.
這件事花了兩個小時才完成。

After all, I _____ at home and helped my dad _____.
結果，我整個下午都待在家裡幫我爸了。

Words

▶ carry 動詞 搬動；搬運　▶ bookshelf 名詞 書架

Grammar Check　It takes *A* + for *B* + to *C*　B 做 C 要花費 A（時間或代價）

前面曾提到 take 具有「花費（時間）」的意思，這裡的「It takes *A* + for *B* + to *C*.」是使用頻率很高的句型，語意為「B 做 C 要花費 A（時間或代價）」，請牢記在心。這個句型有時也會變換成「It takes *B* + *A* + to *C*」。

ex) It takes 30 minutes for me to eat lunch. 我 (B) 吃午餐 (C) 要花 30 分鐘 (A)。
　 = It takes me 30 minutes to eat lunch.

Step 4 自己動手寫寫看
請試著將想到的主題相關內容填進下方空格裡，然後寫出屬於你自己的文章。

Topic
Broken _____

_____, _____, _____

My _____ was/were broken. _____

_____

_____

_____

Learn More　bike

bike 是「腳踏車」和「機車」的縮寫。腳踏車的英文本來是 bicycle，cycle 具有「一個週期；循環」的意思，字首 bi- 則是「2 個」之意，所以 bicycle 其實指的是「2 個的循環」，表示「兩輪的腳踏車」。字首 tri- 具有「3 個」之意，所以「三輪腳踏車」的英文是 tricycle。機車是藉著馬達（motor）的動力來移動，所以英文是 motorcycle。

Day 24　Congratulations! 恭喜！

Step 1　認識核心動詞

congratulate	恭喜	congratulates	congratulated	congratulating
		第三人稱單數現在形	過去形	現在分詞

◼ 恭喜：congratulate＋對象（on＋想要祝賀的事）

I congratulated him on getting a job. 我恭喜他找到工作。

> Tip　congratulations! 表示「恭喜！」，是在想要祝賀對方結婚、畢業、找到工作等事項時經常用到的表達用語，請記得這裡的 congratulation 必須要加上複數字尾的 s。

give	給	gives	gave	giving
		第三人稱單數現在形	過去形	現在分詞

◼ 給～：give＋對象＋物品

Can you give me something to drink?
你可以給我什麼東西喝嗎？

◼ 給～：give＋物品＋to＋對象

He gave a letter to me.
他把一封信給了我。

> Tip　give 的反義詞是 take，而 give and take 通常是「互相讓步」的意思，不過有時也可用來表達「意見交流」的語意。

thank	感謝	thanks	thanked	thanking
		第三人稱單數現在形	過去形	現在分詞

◼ 感謝：thank＋對象（for 想要感謝的事）

He thanked me for my help.
他感謝我的幫助。

> Tip　「Thank you for＋V-ing」也是常用句型，在 Day 16 中介紹過。

124

Step 2　看看別人怎麼寫　請邊聽音檔邊仔細看過一遍，接著再重新唸一遍。

我朋友的鋼琴演奏會
my friend's piano recital

鋼琴彈得非常好
play the piano really well

Topic
Congratulations!

一束花
a bouquet of flowers

感謝
thank

Sunday, September 9, Sunny

I went to see my friend's piano recital today.

He played the piano really well.

After the recital, I congratulated him.

I gave a bouquet of flowers to him.

He thanked me.

我今天去看了我朋友的鋼琴演奏會。
他的鋼琴彈得非常好。
在演奏會結束之後，我恭喜了他。
我給了他一束花。
他向我表示了感謝。

Words

▸ recital 名詞 獨奏會，演奏會　▸ bouquet 名詞 花束　▸ a bouquet of 一束～

125

Step 3 **依樣畫葫蘆** 看一下中文語意，試著使用指定的單字來完成這篇小短文。

I _____ my friend's violin recital today.
我今天去看了我朋友的小提琴演奏會。

She _____ really well.
她的小提琴拉得非常好。

After* the recital, I _____ her.
在演奏會結束之後，我恭喜了她。

I _____ to her.
我給了她一朵向日葵。

She _____ me.
她向我表示了感謝。

Words
▶ **sunflower** 名詞 向日葵

Grammar Check　　after 在～之後

after 在表達與「順序」或「時間」有關的情境時，意思是「在～之後」。不論是句首還是句中，都可以使用 after。

ex) Close the door **after you**.（順序）在你進來之後把門關上。
　　After the rain, the sun came up.（時間）在這場雨之後，太陽出來了。

126

Step 4　自己動手寫寫看　請試著將想到的主題相關內容填進下方空格裡，然後寫出屬於你自己的文章。

Topic
Congratulations!

Learn More　recital / concert / performance

recital 指的是一個人（或一小群人）在舞台上進行演唱或演奏，也就是我們一般會說的「個人獨奏會」或「個人演唱會」，「個人舞蹈表演」也可以用 recital 這個字。concert 指的是「集合多位演奏家或歌手一起表演」的音樂會或演奏會，所以只有由多名演出者一起登台表演的音樂活動才會被稱作 concert。performance 則泛指在觀眾面前進行的演奏或戲劇等表演活動。

Day 25　Eat Out 去外面吃

Step 1　認識核心動詞

decide	決定	decides	decided	deciding
		第三人稱單數現在形	過去形	現在分詞

■ （在 A 與 B 之間）做出決定：**decide (between A and B)**

　You have to decide between yellow and red.　你必須在黃色與紅色之間做出決定。

■ 決定（做什麼）：**decide＋what＋to＋動詞**

　He decided what to eat.　他決定好要吃什麼了。

■ 決定（去做～）：**decide＋to＋動詞**

　We decided to have a meeting.　我們決定要開一個會。

eat	吃	eats	ate	eating
		第三人稱單數現在形	過去形	現在分詞

1 分鐘小教室

雖然都是「進食」的動作，但用英文表達時，「喝水」、「吃飯」和「吃藥」所使用的動詞都各不相同。
drink water 喝水
eat dinner 吃晚餐
take medicine 吃藥

■ 吃

　For your health, you need to eat breakfast every day.
　為了你的健康，你每天都必須吃早餐。

> **Tip** out 是「在外面」的意思，所以 eat out 表示「在外面吃」或「外食」的意思。

drive	① 駕駛 ② 用車載送（人）	drives	drove	driving
		第三人稱單數現在形	過去形	現在分詞

■ 駕駛

　It's dangerous. Drive slowly.　很危險，開慢一點。

■ 用車載送（人）：**drive＋對象＋to＋目的地**

　Can you drive me to school?　你可以開車載我去學校嗎？

128

Step 2 看看別人怎麼寫 請邊聽音檔邊仔細看過一遍，接著再重新唸一遍。

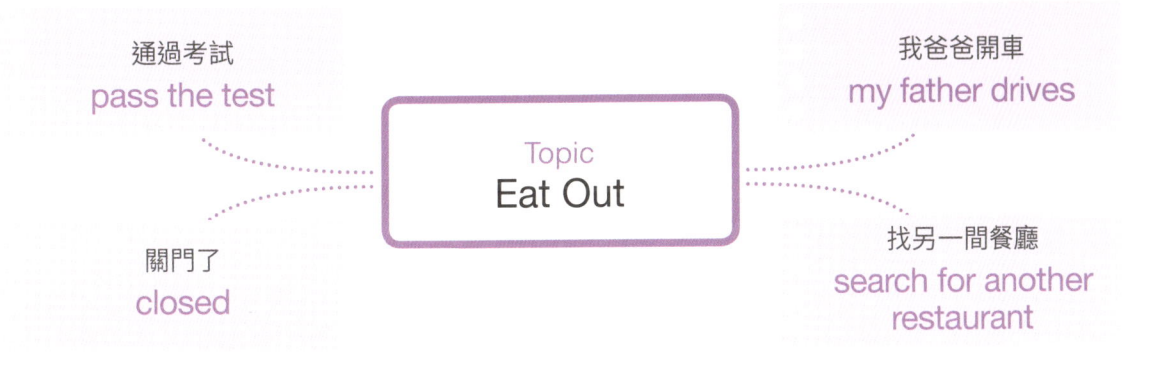

通過考試
pass the test

我爸爸開車
my father drives

Topic
Eat Out

關門了
closed

找另一間餐廳
search for another restaurant

Saturday, April 8, Clear

I passed the Chinese character test.

So my family decided to eat out.

My father drove, and our family went to an Italian restaurant.

But the restaurant was closed.

My dad searched for another restaurant on his phone, and we went there.

我通過了字音字形考試。
所以我們家決定要去外面吃。
我爸爸開車載我們一家去了一間義大利餐廳。
但那間餐廳沒開。
我爸爸用他的手機找了另一間餐廳，然後我們就去了那裡。

Words

▶ pass 動詞 通過　▶ Chinese 名詞 中文　▶ character 名詞 文字　▶ Chinese character 中文字
▶ so 連接詞 所以　▶ search for 尋找～，搜尋～　▶ another 形容詞 另一個的　▶ there 副詞 那裡

Step 3 依樣畫葫蘆　看一下中文語意，試著使用指定的單字來完成這篇小短文。

I passed the _____.
我通過了電腦證照考試。

So my family _____.
所以我們家決定要去外面吃。

_____, and our family went to _____.
我媽媽開車載我們一家去了一間中式餐廳。

But the restaurant was _____.
但那間餐廳還沒開門。

My dad _____ another* restaurant on his phone, and we went there.
我爸爸用他的手機找了另一間餐廳，然後我們就去了那裡。

Words

▸ certification 名詞 證明；證照　▸ open 形容詞 營業中的　▸ yet 副詞 還沒，尚未

Grammar Check　another 另一個（的）

another 是由 an（一個）跟 other（其他的）結合而成的單字，表示「另一個（的）」。當本來要去的「那間餐廳（the restaurant）」沒開時，所搜尋的是「另一間」餐廳，所以會用 another 來表達。

ex) Would you like **another** drink?　你想再來一杯飲料嗎？

Step 4　自己動手寫寫看　請試著將想到的主題相關內容填進下方空格裡，然後寫出屬於你自己的文章。

Topic
Eat Out

..................., ..., ...

So my family decided to eat out.

Learn More　find / look for / search

動詞（片語）find、look for 和 search 都是「尋找」的意思，但三者所想表達的語意略有不同。find 指的是像在玩捉迷藏般地「（可能是碰巧）成功找到」；look for 描述的則是在日常生活中「試圖找到某個東西的動作或過程」，但不一定最後有成功找到；search 則帶有為了尋找某個東西而「仔細又專注地查找」的意思，因此若想描述「用手機或電腦搜尋」時，必須使用 search 這個字。

Review Test 5 (Day 21~25)

A 請寫出與以下中文相對應的英文動詞。

1. 搭乘（交通工具）；花費（時間等） → take
2. 說話；談論 → t_____
3. 恭喜 → c_____
4. 聆聽；聽從 → l_____
5. 吃 → e_____
6. 感受（情緒等）；（透過觸摸來）感受 → f_____
7. 暫留；停留 → s_____
8. 油漆；塗上顏色 → p_____
9. 收集；使集合 → c_____
10. 駕駛；用車載送（人） → d_____
11. 呼叫，喊叫；打電話 → c_____
12. 感謝 → t_____
13. 轉向；使轉動 → t_____
14. 決定 → d_____
15. 給 → g_____

B 請將英文單字與相對應的中文意思連起來。

1. hobby •   • ⓐ 最喜歡的
2. finish •   • ⓑ 腳踏車；機車
3. spend •   • ⓒ 獨奏會，演奏會
4. recital •   • ⓓ 完成；結束
5. favorite •   • ⓔ 覺得無聊的
6. bike •   • ⓕ 嗜好，興趣
7. character •   • ⓖ 文字
8. pass •   • ⓗ 花費（時間）；花（錢）
9. bored •   • ⓘ 花束
10. bouquet •   • ⓙ 通過

132

C 請根據中文句意將適當的字詞填入空格之中，完成英文句子。

1. In the end, I spent my time __tidying up my room__.
   最後，我把時間拿來整理我的房間了。

2. I _____ easy dances _____ watching the music video.
   我在看 MV（音樂錄影帶）時會一邊試著跳簡單的舞步。

3. I hit the wall while _____ and it broke.
   我在搬書架的時候撞到了牆，結果書架就壞了。

4. She _____ really well.
   她的小提琴拉得很棒。

5. I passed the _____.
   我通過了電腦證照考試。

D 請利用下列提示的英文動詞來寫出符合中文句意的英文句子。

1. feel   I felt bored all day.
   我一整天都覺得很無聊。

2. collect _____
   我的嗜好是收集我最喜歡的歌手的專輯。

3. take _____
   這項工作花了兩個小時來完成。

4. give _____
   我給了我朋友一束花。

5. decide, eat _____
   我們一家決定去外面吃。

Week 6

Day 26 **cook, sit, see** ▶ 去露營

Day 27 **want, pay** ▶ 文具店

Day 28 **fight, tell, answer** ▶ 跟朋友吵架

Day 29 **make, look** ▶ 新毛衣

Day 30 **take, study, get** ▶ 數學測驗

Review Test 6

Day 26　Go Camping 去露營

Step 1　認識核心動詞

cook	料理，烹飪	**cook**s 第三人稱單數現在形	**cook**ed 過去形	**cook**ing 現在分詞

■ 料理，烹飪

　Dad cooked while Mom cleaned.　爸爸在媽媽打掃時做了飯。

■ 為～料理～：**cook**＋食物＋**for**＋對象

　He cooks fried rice for his son every week.　他每週都會為他的兒子做炒飯。

sit	坐	**sit**s 第三人稱單數現在形	**sat** 過去形	**sit**ting 現在分詞

■ 坐：**sit**＋**on/in**＋物品

　She sat on a chair.　她坐在了椅子上。

＊通常會用 on，但如果是「整個人陷進去、癱坐在扶手椅或沙發上」時，就要用 in。

Tip stand：站立　＊過去形是 stood

　　He is *standing* in front of the school.　他正站在學校前面。

see	① 看見，看到 ② 理解，知道	**see**s 第三人稱單數現在形	**saw** 過去形	**see**ing 現在分詞

■ 看見，看到

　I went to see the sea with my wife.　我跟我老婆一起去看海了。

■ 理解，知道

　Oh, I see.　噢，我懂了。

＊這個表達方式比較常用在對話之中，寫作時較少用到。

Step 2　看看別人怎麼寫　請邊聽音檔邊仔細看過一遍，接著再重新唸一遍。

在海灘
at the beach

煮晚餐
cook dinner

Topic
Go Camping

圍坐在營火旁聊天
sit around the campfire and talk

看星星
see the stars

Friday, June 29, Warm

My family went camping at the beach.

I cooked dinner with my dad.

We sat around the campfire and talked.

We saw the stars in the night sky.

My family went to bed around 12 o'clock.

我們家去了海灘露營。
我跟爸爸一起煮了晚餐。
我們圍坐在營火旁聊天。
我們在夜空中看到了星星。
我們家在 12 點鐘左右就去睡了。

Words

▶ around 介系詞 在～周圍 副詞 周圍；大約　▶ campfire 名詞 營火

Step 3　依樣畫葫蘆　看一下中文語意，試著使用指定的單字來完成這篇小短文。

My family went camping _____.
我們家去了山谷裡露營。

I _____ with my dad.
我跟爸爸一起煮了晚餐。

We _____ * the campfire and _____ marshmallows.
我們圍坐在營火旁烤棉花糖。

We _____ in the night sky.
我們在夜空中看到了月亮。

My family _____ around* 12 o'clock.
我們家在 12 點鐘左右就去睡了。

Words

- valley 名詞 山谷
- in the valley 在山谷裡
- roast 動詞（直接放在火源上或串成串）火烤
- moon 名詞 月亮

Grammar Check　around 在～周圍；大約

around 可用來表達「時間」或「地點」，用在描述時間時，意思是「大約～」或「將近～」，用來描述地點時，則會是「在～周圍」的意思。

ex) Look around the room. 環視房間。

Step 4 自己動手寫寫看　請試著將想到的主題相關內容填進下方空格裡，然後寫出屬於你自己的文章。

Topic
Go Camping

_____, _____,

My family went camping _____

Learn More　跟露營（camping）有關的表達用語

1. Can you help me pitch the tent? 你能幫我把帳篷搭起來嗎？
2. We need to put up a mosquito net. 我們得架個蚊帳。
3. Let's grill the meat. 我們來烤肉吧。
4. camper van 露營車
5. camping site 露營區
6. glamping 豪華露營
   * 不用自行準備帳篷、食物或炊具等用品，只要直接到已備好所需一切的地點，享受露營樂趣的一種露營方式。

Day 27　Stationery Store 文具店

Step 1　認識核心動詞

want	① 要 ② 想要 ③ 希望	wants	wanted	wanting
		第三人稱單數現在形	過去形	現在分詞

■ 要

Do you **want** some tea?　你要喝點茶嗎？
What do you **want**?　你想要什麼？

■ 想要（做～）：**want＋to＋動詞**

She **wants to meet** her mother.　她想要和她的媽媽見面。

■ 希望（～去做～）：**want＋對象＋to＋動詞**

Mom **wants me to study**.　媽媽希望我去讀書。

pay	支付	pays	paid	paying
		第三人稱單數現在形	過去形	現在分詞

■ 支付：**pay＋金額／pay＋for＋物品或服務**

I **paid** 2,000 dollars.　我付了 2,000 元。
I will **pay for** the ticket.　我會付這個票的錢。

■（以～）支付：**pay＋with＋支付方式**

Can I **pay with** a credit card?　我可以用信用卡付嗎？

> **Tip** pay 做為名詞時，除了「支付」以外，也有「薪水」或「報酬」的意思。

Step 2 看看別人怎麼寫 請邊聽音檔邊仔細看過一遍，接著再重新唸一遍。

想要一本筆記本
want a notebook

走去文具店
walk to the stationery store

Topic
Stationery Store

付台幣 200 元
pay 200 NTD

拿回台幣 50 元
get 50 NTD back

Tuesday, March 4, Windy

A new semester began this week.

I wanted to buy a notebook.

I walked to the stationery store.

I asked the owner where the notebook was.

It was 150 NTD. I paid 200 NTD and got 50 NTD back.

新學期這週開始了。
我想要買一本筆記本。
我走去了文具店。
我問了老闆筆記本放在哪裡。
筆記本是台幣 150 元。我付了台幣 200 元，拿回了台幣 50 元。

Words

▸ semester 名詞 學期　▸ begin 動詞 開始 *過去形是 began　▸ stationery 名詞 文具
▸ owner 名詞 老闆；擁有者　▸ ask 動詞 問，詢問　▸ get back 拿回

141

Step 3 依樣畫葫蘆　看一下中文語意，試著使用指定的單字來完成這篇小短文。

A new semester _____.
新學期這個月開始了。

I _____ buy _____.
我想要買色鉛筆。

I walked to the _____.
我走去了文具店。

I asked the owner where the* _____ were.
我問了老闆色鉛筆放在哪裡。

They were 550 NTD.
色鉛筆是台幣 550 元。

I _____ 1,000 NTD and _____ 450 NTD
_____.
我付了台幣 1,000 元，拿回了台幣 450 元。

Words

▶ month 名詞 （一年 12 個月中的一個）月，月份　▶ colored pencil 名詞 色鉛筆

Grammar Check　提及前面出現過的名詞時，會使用 the

當提及前面出現過的名詞時，就會使用有限定範圍效果的 the。在第一次提到想買色鉛筆時，因為心中還不確定想要買哪種色鉛筆，所以會說沒有限定範圍的 colored pencils（表達單數時會用 a colored pencil），但在問老闆色鉛筆放在哪裡時，指的是有限定範圍的「特定想買的那些色鉛筆」，因此會用 the colored pencils 來表達。

ex) There is an apple. 有一顆蘋果。→ The apple is delicious. 這顆蘋果很好吃。

Step 4　自己動手寫寫看　請試著將想到的主題相關內容填進下方空格裡，然後寫出屬於你自己的文章。

Topic
Stationery Store

＿＿＿＿＿＿＿, ＿＿＿＿＿＿, ＿＿＿＿＿

I wanted to buy ＿＿＿＿＿＿＿＿＿＿＿＿＿＿＿

Learn More　　stationery 的由來

雖然現在經常會用電腦或電子裝置來取代文具，但在過去沒有這些設備的時代，日常生活中多半會使用文具，因此據說在火車站周圍總是會有文具店，讓大家可以輕鬆買到文具。火車站的英文是 station，而文具的英文 stationery 便是源自於此。

1. ruler（量長度用的）尺
2. scissors 剪刀
3. glue 膠水
4. brush 筆刷
5. eraser 橡皮擦
6. pencil holder 筆筒

Day 28 Fighting with a Friend 跟朋友吵架

Step 1 認識核心動詞

fight	打架；爭吵	fights	fought	fighting
		第三人稱單數現在形	過去形	現在分詞

▨ （跟～）打架；爭吵：**fight＋with＋對象**

I **fought with Jane** yesterday and apologized to her today.
我昨天跟 Jane 吵架，所以今天向她道歉。

▨ （為～而）打架；爭吵：**fight＋about＋主題**

We **fought about classroom cleaning**. 我們因為教室清潔的事而爭吵。

> **Tip** make up with：跟～和好
> I tried to *make up with* my friend. 我努力要和朋友和好。

tell	說；告訴；吩咐	tells	told	telling
		第三人稱單數現在形	過去形	現在分詞

▨ 說；告訴：**tell＋對象＋內容／tell＋內容＋to＋對象**

He **told me the truth**. ＝ He **told the truth to me**.
他告訴了我真相。＝他把真相告訴了我。

▨ 吩咐（～去做～）：**tell＋對象＋to＋動作**

I **told her to come** right away. 我吩咐了她立刻過來。

answer	① 回答 ② 回應	answers	answered	answering
		第三人稱單數現在形	過去形	現在分詞

▨ 回答

Who can **answer** the question? 誰可以回答這個問題？

▨ 回應

I knocked on the door but no one **answered**. 我敲了門，但無人回應。

144

Step 2 看看別人怎麼寫 請邊聽音檔邊仔細看過一遍，接著再重新唸一遍。

玩了一個桌遊
play a board game

遵守遊戲規則
follow the game rules

Topic
Fighting with a Friend

生氣的
angry

退一步
yield

Wednesday, November 22, Cold

Today I felt bad because I had a fight with my friend.

I played a board game with my friend.

But he didn't follow the game rules. I was angry and fought with him.

Mom told me to yield and said a proverb, "A friend is a second self."

I reluctantly answered, "Yes, I will."

我今天心情不好，因為我跟朋友吵架了。
我跟朋友一起玩了一個桌遊。
但他沒有遵守遊戲規則。我很生氣，然後就和他吵架了。
媽媽叫我要退一步，還說了一句俗語：「朋友就像是另一個自己。」
我不情願地回答：「好吧，我會的。」

Words

▶ fight 名詞 打架；爭吵　▶ follow 動詞 遵守；跟隨；接在～之後　▶ yield 動詞 退一步；屈服
▶ proverb 名詞 諺語，俗語　▶ reluctantly 副詞 不情願地；勉強地

145

Step 3 **依樣畫葫蘆** 看一下中文語意，試著使用指定的單字來完成這篇小短文。

Today I _____ because I had a fight with my friend.
我今天心情不好，因為我跟朋友吵架了。

I _____ with my _____.
我跟朋友一起打了棒球。

But _____ didn't _____ the game rules.
但他們之中有一個人不遵守比賽規則。

I was _____ and* _____ him.
我被他惹到發火，然後就和他吵架了。

Mom _____ me _____ yield and said a _____, "A friend is a second self."
媽媽叫我要退一步，還說了一句諺語：「朋友就像是另一個自己。」

I reluctantly _____, "Yes, I will."
我不情願地回答：「好吧，我會的。」

Words

▶ irritated 形容詞 被惹火的，生氣的

Grammar Check　　and 然後；而且

and 是用來連接兩個句子的連接詞，當前後兩句的主詞相同時，後句的主詞可省略。

ex) I was angry. + I fought with him. → I was angry and fought with him.
　　我很生氣，然後和他吵架了。

Step 4　自己動手寫寫看　請試著將想到的主題相關內容填進下方空格裡，然後寫出屬於你自己的文章。

Topic
Fighting with a Friend

_____, _____, _____

Today I _____ because

Learn More　跟「友情」有關的英文俗語

1. **An old friend is better than two new ones.**　一個老朋友勝過兩個新朋友。
   * *A* better than *B*：A 勝過 B
2. **A friend in need is a friend indeed.**　患難見真情。
   * in need 有困難時　* indeed 副詞 真正地，確實

147

Day 29　New Sweater 新毛衣

Step 1　認識核心動詞

make	① 做；製造 ② 使～做～	makes	made	making
		第三人稱單數現在形	過去形	現在分詞

■ （運用～）做～；製造～：**make＋物品＋from／of＋材料**

Our company makes toys of plastic.　我們公司製造塑膠玩具。

■ （為～）製作～：**make＋物品＋for＋對象**

I made a cake for her.　我為她做了一個蛋糕。

■ 製作～（給～）：**make＋對象＋物品**

Mom made me a shirt.　媽媽做了一件襯衫給我。

■ 使～做～：**make＋對象＋動詞**

The photo made her laugh.　這張照片讓她大笑了。

> **Tip** make 的字義及用途又多又廣，這裡提到的只是其中幾個，請一定要好好查字典確認字義和正確用法。

look	① 看 ② 看起來	looks	looked	looking
		第三人稱單數現在形	過去形	現在分詞

■ 看：**look at**

Look at the blackboard.　請看黑板。

■ 看起來～

What's going on? You look sad.　怎麼了？你看起來很難過。

■ 看起來（像 A）：**look like＋A**

The photo doesn't look like her.　這張照片看起來不像她。

148

Step 2　看看別人怎麼寫　請邊聽音檔邊仔細看過一遍，接著再重新唸一遍。

MP3-029

我媽媽製作　my mom makes

試穿　try on

Topic
New Sweater

看起來很棒　look nice

發照片　post the photo

Monday, December 24, Snowy

My mom made me a sweater.

I tried on the sweater.

It looked nice and good on me.

I took a selfie. I posted it on my SNS account.

Many friends saw the photo and clicked the like button.

我媽媽做了一件毛衣給我。
我試穿了那件毛衣。
它看起來很棒，而且在我身上很好看。
我拍了一張自拍。我把照片發在了我的社群帳號上。
很多朋友看到了這張照片，然後按了讚。

Words

- **try on** 試穿，試戴
- **look good on** 在～的身上很好看
- **selfie** 名詞 自拍
- **take a selfie** 拍了一張自拍
- **post** 動詞 張貼；發布
- **SNS** Social Network Service 的縮寫（能在網路上和他人建立關係或交流的「社群網路服務」）
- **account** 名詞 帳號

Step 3 依樣畫葫蘆 看一下中文語意，試著使用指定的單字來完成這篇小短文。

My mom _____ me _____.
我媽媽做了一件洋裝給我。

I _____* the dress.
我試穿了那件洋裝。

It _____ and _____ me.
它看起來很漂亮，而且在我身上很好看。

I _____. I _____ it on my SNS account.
我拍了一張自拍。我把它上傳到了我的社群帳號上。

Many friends saw the photo and wrote _____.
很多朋友看到了這張照片，然後留了言。

Words

▶ pretty 形容詞 漂亮的　▶ upload 動詞 上傳　▶ comment 名詞 評論；留言

Grammar Check　　try on 試穿，試戴

因為 try 的意思是「嘗試做做看」，且 on 的基本語意是「接觸」，所以 try on 的直譯就是「嘗試接觸看看」，也就有了「試穿（衣服、鞋子等）」或「試戴（手套等）」的語意。

ex) Try on this hat. 試戴看看這頂帽子。
　　I'll try on this jacket. 我會試穿看看這件夾克。

Step 4 自己動手寫寫看
請試著將想到的主題相關內容填進下方空格裡，然後寫出屬於你自己的文章。

Topic: New _____

_____, _____, _____
_____ made me

Learn More　SNS（Social 社交的 Networks 關係網路 Service 服務）

對於 SNS 一詞，不同國家或不同學者之間所下的定義都各不相同，但均有著「於線上空間進行、建立人際關係及共享資訊」的共通點，目前最具代表性的 SNS 有 Facebook、X、Instagram 和 Threads 等等。雖然 SNS 具有可與他人快速溝通交流的優點，但也存在著個資外洩或成癮等風險，因此使用時應具備正確的觀念與知識。

Day 30　Math Test 數學測驗

Step 1　認識核心動詞

take	① 參加（考試） ② 拍攝（照片）	take**s** 第三人稱單數現在形	**took** 過去形	tak**ing** 現在分詞

1 分鐘小教室

我們在前面曾說過 take 擁有多種語意，現在要介紹的則是與 take 的基本語意「抓」相關的字義。「抓住眼前的考卷」表示「參加（考試）」，「抓住相機」則表示「拍攝（照片）」的意思。

▨ 參加（考試）

He **took** a science test today.
他今天考了自然。

▨ 拍攝（照片）

I **took** pictures in the park.
我在公園裡拍了照。

study	學習	stud**ies** 第三人稱單數現在形	stud**ied** 過去形	study**ing** 現在分詞

▨ 學習

He **studies** English every day.　他每天都會念英文。

▨ （為～）學習：**study＋for＋目的**

I **studied** for the exam.　我為了這次考試念書。

get	① 收到 ② 得到	get**s** 第三人稱單數現在形	**got** 過去形	get**ting** 現在分詞

▨ 收到

I **got** a birthday present.　我收到了一份生日禮物。

▨ 得到

I **got** good information from my friend.　我從我朋友那邊得到了有用的資訊。

Step 2 看看別人怎麼寫 請邊聽音檔邊仔細看過一遍，接著再重新唸一遍。

參加考試
take a test

有信心的
confident

Topic
Math Test

困難的
difficult

低分
low score

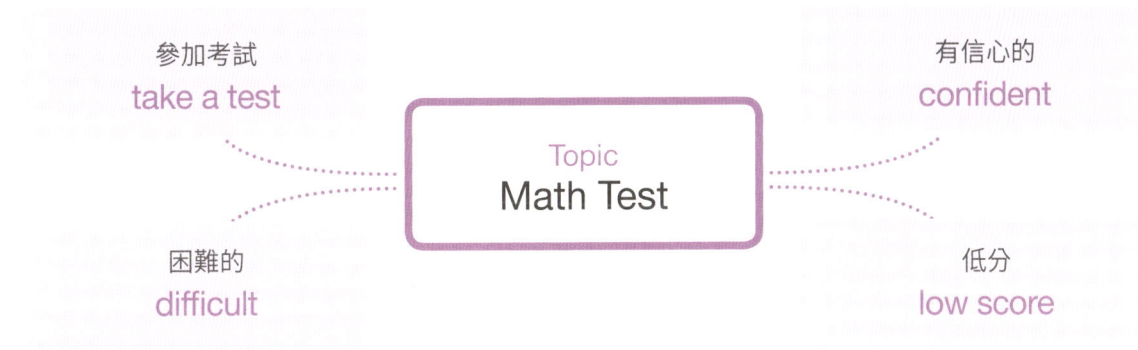

Thursday, July 12, Hot

I **took** a math test today.

I was confident because I **studied** it hard.

But the problems were difficult.

I couldn't solve all the problems in time.

In the end, I **got** a low score.

我今天考了數學。
我很有信心，因為我念得很認真。
可是那些題目很難。
我來不及寫完所有的題目。
最後，我拿了低分。

Words

▶ confident 形容詞 有信心的　▶ in time 及時　▶ low 形容詞 低的　▶ score 名詞 分數

Step 3　依樣畫葫蘆　看一下中文語意，試著使用指定的單字來完成這篇小短文。

I _____ test today.
我今天考了自然。

I had _____ because I _____ it hard.
我沒在擔心，因為我念得很認真。

But the problems were _____.
可是那些題目很陌生。

I couldn't* _____ in time.
我來不及寫完所有的題目。

In the end, I _____ a low score.
最後，我拿了低分。

Words

▸ worry 名詞 擔心　動詞 擔心　▸ unfamiliar 形容詞 陌生的；不熟悉的

Grammar Check　could 表達「過去的能力」或「有禮貌的請求」

could 有很多意思，其中最常表達的是「過去的能力」，正如同上方短文就用了 could，來描述「當時及時寫完題目的能力」。第二常見的則是「有禮貌的請求」，例如 Can you help me?（你可以幫我嗎？），若改用 could 變成 Could you help me?，句意就變成更有禮貌的「請問您可以幫我嗎？」。此外，could 也能用來表達「可能性」，請記得此時的 could 並非單純是 can 的過去形。

Step 4　自己動手寫寫看　請試著將想到的主題相關內容填進下方空格裡，然後寫出屬於你自己的文章。

Topic
_____ Test

_____, _____, _____

I took a _____ test today. _____

Learn More　跟「考試」有關的表達用語

1. **cram for** 為～臨時抱佛腳
   ex) I'm cramming for the test. 我正在為這場考試臨時抱佛腳。
2. **run out of** ～不夠；～用完　ex) I ran out of time. 我時間用完了。
3. **Good luck on your test.** 祝你考試順利。
4. **stay up all night** 整晚沒睡，熬了一整個晚上

155

Review Test 6 (Day 26~30)

A 請根據中文正確排列英文字母並將相對應的英文動詞填入框中。

	中文	字母	答案
1	要；想要；希望	awtn	want
2	回答；回應	wsnear	
3	看；看起來	olko	
4	打架；爭吵	gitfh	
5	參加（考試）；拍攝（照片）	ekat	
6	坐	its	
7	做；製造；使～做～	kame	
8	看見，看到；理解，知道	ees	
9	支付	ayp	
10	收到；得到	egt	
11	料理，烹飪	koco	
12	學習	dutsy	
13	說；告訴；吩咐	letl	

B 請找到跟中文相對應的英文單字並標示出來，然後把單字填入空格之中。

```
t a e w n n e f s d
c s r f o i j g u l
a i n o f l b u s e
m y s l u k l e f i
p f e c g n m o c y
f s m u o e d t f z
i q s w s r e n w o
r s k t q o e k q o
e g e a c c o u n t
i r m t l o w g d n
```

	中文	答案
1	在～周圍；大約	around
2	營火	c_____
3	學期	s_____
4	老闆；擁有者	o_____
5	遵守；跟隨；接在～之後	f_____
6	退一步；屈服	y_____
7	自拍	s_____
8	帳號	a_____
9	低的	l_____
10	分數	s_____

C 請根據中文句意將適當的字詞填入空格之中，完成英文句子。

1. My family went camping _____in the valley._____.
   我們家去了山谷裡露營。

2. I walked to the _____.
   我走路去了文具店。

3. I _____ with my _____.
   我跟朋友一起打了棒球。

4. I _____ it on my SNS account.
   我把它上傳到了我的社群帳號上。

5. I couldn't _____ in time.
   我來不及寫完所有的題目。

D 請利用下列提示的英文字詞來寫出符合中文句意的英文句子。

1. _____I cooked dinner with my dad._____
   我跟爸爸一起煮了晚餐。　　　　　(dad / I / with / my / dinner / cooked)

2. _____
   我想要買一本筆記本。　　　　　(notebook / I / a / buy / to / wanted)

3. _____
   我很生氣，然後就和我朋友吵架了。　(with / and / I / angry / my / was / fought / friend)

4. _____
   我媽媽做了一件毛衣給我。　　　　(made / My / sweater / me / a / mom)

5. _____
   我今天考了數學。　　　　　　　(today / I / math / test / took / a)

157

Week 7

Day 31 **wash, break, say** ▶ 做家事

Day 32 **understand, cry, solve** ▶ 念數學

Day 33 **plan, save, hope** ▶ 存錢

Day 34 **live, move, miss** ▶ 搬家跟轉學

Day 35 **run, fall, end** ▶ 跑步

Review Test 7

Day 31　Doing Housework 做家事

Step 1　認識核心動詞

wash	① 清洗；洗澡 ② 洗衣服	wash**es** 第三人稱單數現在形	wash**ed** 過去形	wash**ing** 現在分詞

■ 清洗；洗澡

I sweated and washed my body clean. 我流了汗，所以去洗了澡。

■ 洗衣服

I washed my pants because they were dirty. 我洗了我的長褲，因為它們很髒。

break	① 打破，打碎；弄壞 ② 破損；壞掉，故障	break**s** 第三人稱單數現在形	broke 過去形	break**ing** 現在分詞

1 分鐘小教室

break 最基本的意思是「打破（物品）」，且從這個字義擴大衍生出了其他多種語意，例如「打破法律」表示「違法」，「打破紀錄」表示「改寫紀錄」，「打破機器裝置」則是「故障，壞掉」的意思。如果想要表達「打破沉默」，也可以用 break 這個字。

■ 打破，打碎；弄壞（物品）

He broke the safe and stole the money.
他弄壞了保險箱把錢偷走。

■ 打破（紀錄）

The runner broke the world record.
那位跑者打破了世界紀錄。

■ 破損；壞掉，故障

I couldn't watch soccer because the TV broke.
我因為電視壞掉而無法看足球了。

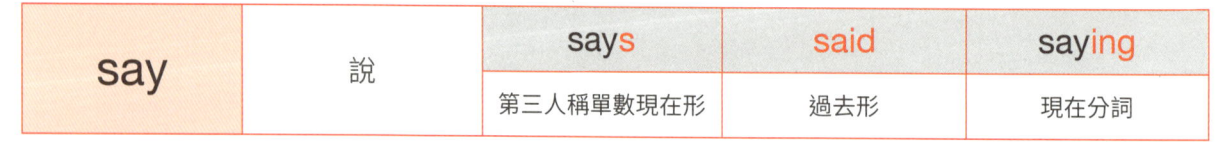

say	說	say**s** 第三人稱單數現在形	said 過去形	say**ing** 現在分詞

■ 說：say＋內容＋to＋對象

She said hello to me. 她向我打了招呼。

Step 2 看看別人怎麼寫 請邊聽音檔邊仔細看過一遍，接著再重新唸一遍。

洗碗
wash the dishes

掉了一個盤子
miss a dish

Topic
Doing Housework

嚇一跳的
startled

小心
be careful

Tuesday, September 25, Foggy

I was washing the dishes.

I missed a dish and it broke.

I was startled, and my mom came to me.

My mom asked me, "Are you okay?" I said to my mom, "I'm okay."

She told me to be careful next time.

我那時正在洗碗。
我掉了一個盤子，結果它破了。
我嚇了一跳，然後我媽媽就過來我這裡了。
媽媽問我：「你沒事吧？」。我跟媽媽說：「我沒事。」
她叫我下次要小心一點。

Words

- miss 動詞 遺漏；未抓住
- startled 形容詞 吃驚的，嚇一跳的
- careful 形容詞 小心的
- next time 下次

Step 3 **依樣畫葫蘆** 看一下中文語意，試著使用指定的單字來完成這篇小短文。

I was _____.
我那時正在洗碗。

I _____ and it _____.
我掉了一個碗，結果它破了。

I was _____, and my mom came to me.
我覺得很丟臉，然後我媽媽就過來我這裡了。

My mom asked me, "Are you all _____?"
媽媽問我：「你沒事吧？」。

I _____ my mom, "I'm okay."
我跟媽媽說：「我沒事。」

She told me to be* _____ next time.
她叫我下次要小心一點。

Words

▶ bowl 名詞 碗　▶ embarrassed 形容詞 覺得丟臉的；難為情的

Grammar Check　to be ＋形容詞（或名詞）

在 Day 28 學過「tell ＋對象＋to ＋動作」的表達方式，此時的 to 後面應該要接動詞，但由於 careful 是形容詞，不能直接放在 to 的後方，所以 to 後面要先接 be 再接 careful。

ex) She told me **to be happy**.（形容詞）她叫我要開心一點。
　　She told me **to be a doctor**.（名詞）她叫我要當醫生。

Step 4　自己動手寫寫看　請試著將想到的主題相關內容填進下方空格裡，然後寫出屬於你自己的文章。

Topic
Doing Housework

Learn More　跟「家事」有關的表達用語

1. **separate the trash** 垃圾分類
2. **do the laundry** 洗衣服
3. **fold the clothes** 摺衣服
4. **vacuum** 用吸塵器
5. **wipe** 擦乾淨

Day 32　Math Study 念數學

Step 1　認識核心動詞

understand	理解，懂得	understands	understood	understanding
		第三人稱單數現在形	過去形	現在分詞

▨ 理解，懂得

Can you *understand* Japanese?　你會（懂得）日文嗎？

Tip misunderstand：誤解；誤會

　　Don't *misunderstand* me.　請別誤會我。

cry	① 哭泣 ② 喊叫	cries	cried	crying
		第三人稱單數現在形	過去形	現在分詞

▨ （因為～而）哭泣：**cry＋over/about/for＋原因**

It is no use *crying over spilt milk*.
（英文俗語）為打翻的牛奶哭泣是沒有用的。（覆水難收）

▨ 喊叫：**cry out**（for＋原因）

I *cried out* his name.　我喊出了他的名字。
She *cried out* for help.　她大聲呼救。

solve	解決；解答	solves	solved	solving
		第三人稱單數現在形	過去形	現在分詞

▨ 解決；解答：**solve＋a problem**（問題）**/a puzzle**（謎題）**/a riddle**（謎語）

He is good at *solving puzzles*.
他擅長解謎。

164

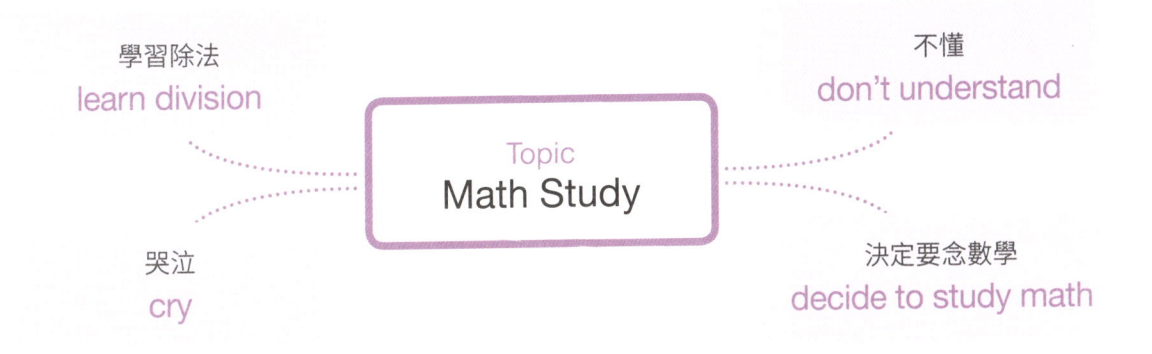

Step 2　看看別人怎麼寫　請邊聽音檔邊仔細看過一遍，接著再重新唸一遍。

學習除法
learn division

不懂
don't understand

Topic
Math Study

哭泣
cry

決定要念數學
decide to study math

Friday, March 10, Cloudy

I learned division today.

However, I was upset because I didn't understand the class content.

I came home and cried.

But soon, I didn't think crying would solve the problem.

I decided to study math for 30 minutes every day.

我今天學了除法。
可是，我覺得很煩，因為我聽不懂上課內容。
我回到家哭了。
但很快，我覺得哭不能解決問題。
我決定每天要念 30 分鐘的數學。

Words

▶ division 名詞 除法　▶ upset 形容詞 心煩的，苦惱的　▶ content 名詞 內容　▶ every day 每天

Step 3 依樣畫葫蘆　看一下中文語意，試著使用指定的單字來完成這篇小短文。

I learned _____ today.
我今天學了長方形。

However, I was _____ because I _____ the class content.
可是，我覺得很煩躁，因為我聽不懂上課內容。

I came home and _____.
我回到家哭了。

But soon, I didn't think crying would* _____.
但很快，我覺得哭不能解決問題。

I decided to _____ for 30 minutes every day.
我決定每天要複習課程 30 分鐘。

Words

▶ rectangle 名詞 長方形　▶ irritated 形容詞 煩躁的；被激怒的　▶ review 動詞 複習；再檢查
▶ lesson 名詞 課程

Grammar Check　時態一致

仔細觀察「我覺得哭不能解決問題」這句中文，會發現「我覺得～」是在那時的感受，也就是發生在過去的事，「解決問題」則是尚未發生的未來之事，兩件事的時態並不相同。另一方面，出現在英文句子裡的兩個動詞的時態必須一致，因此即使「解決問題」是發生在未來的某個時間點，但因為「我覺得～」的發生時間點在過去，所以必須配合將「解決問題」的時態從 will 改成過去形 would 才行。

Step 4　自己動手寫寫看　請試著將想到的主題相關內容填進下方空格裡，然後寫出屬於你自己的文章。

Topic
_____ Study

_____, _____, _____

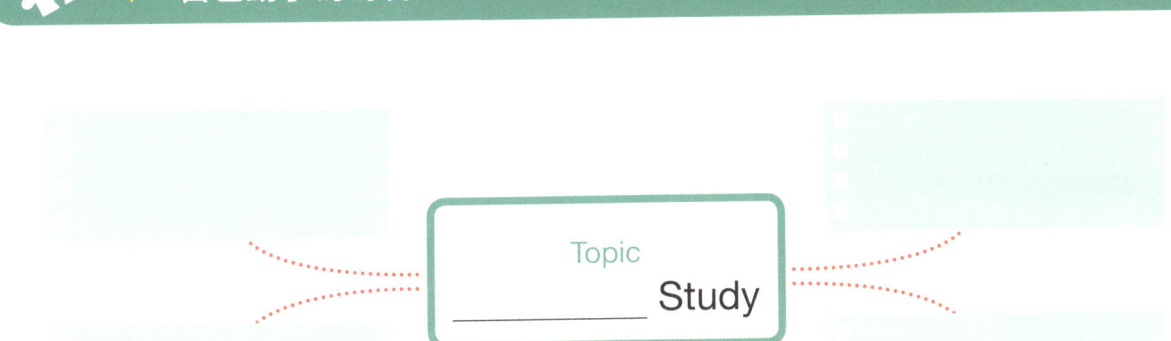

I learned _____

Learn More　單字小故事 ❹ under（在～下方）

你知道「underground 樂團」指的是什麼樣的樂團嗎？underground 這個字是由 under（在～下方）跟 ground（地面）所構成，因此指的是「沒有在主流媒體上出道、以線下現場表演為主」的樂團。此外，understand 是「under（在～下方）＋stand（站立）」→「站在（理解範圍）下方」，因此是「理解」的意思。另一方面，underline 則是「under（在～下方）＋line（畫線）」→「在（文字）下方畫線」，表達出「強調」的字義。

Day 33 Saving Money 存錢

Step 1 認識核心動詞

| plan | ① 計劃；打算（做某件事）
② 制定計畫，規劃 | plans
第三人稱單數現在形 | planned
過去形 | planning
現在分詞 |

■ 計劃；打算（做某件事）：**plan＋to＋動詞**

I'm planning to travel to America. 我正在計劃要去美國。

■ 為～制定計畫，規劃～：**plan＋for＋需要規劃的事項**

My family planned for camping. 我們一家規劃了露營的事。

| save | ① 存～
② 拯救，挽救 | saves
第三人稱單數現在形 | saved
過去形 | saving
現在分詞 |

■ 存～：**save (up)＋對象＋for＋目的**

She saved money for the trip. 她為這趟旅行存了錢。

■ 拯救；挽救：**save＋對象＋from＋危難**

The 119 crew saved people from the flood. 119 救難人員從洪水中救出了人們。

| hope | 希望 | hopes
第三人稱單數現在形 | hoped
過去形 | hoping
現在分詞 |

1 分鐘小教室

hope 帶有「期盼某件事發生」的語意。如果在英文字典裡查找 wish 這個字，就會發現雖然 wish 也是「希望」，但通常描述的是「發生可能性不高」或「不可能發生」的事。

■ 希望：**hope＋to＋動詞**

I hope to see her next week.
我希望下週能見到她。

■ 希望：**hope＋(that)＋主詞＋動詞**

I hope South Korea wins the soccer match.
我希望韓國能贏下這場足球比賽。

Step 2 看看別人怎麼寫 請邊聽音檔邊仔細看過一遍，接著再重新唸一遍。

Topic: Saving Money

- 我最喜歡的歌手的演唱會 — my favorite singer's concert
- 昂貴的票 — expensive ticket
- 沒有足夠的錢 — don't have enough money
- 存錢 — save up money

Saturday, February 2, Rainy

I plan to go to my favorite singer's concert.

However, the ticket price is expensive at 10,000 NTD.

I don't have enough money to buy the ticket.

I'm saving up money to buy it.

I hope I can save money before the concert.

我打算要去我最喜歡的歌手的演唱會。
不過，票價貴到要台幣 10,000 元。
我沒有足夠的錢可以買票。
我正在存錢要買票。
我希望能在演唱會之前存到錢。

Words

- expensive 形容詞 昂貴的
- at 介系詞 以～（某種價格或速度等）
- enough 形容詞 足夠的

Step 3　依樣畫葫蘆　看一下中文語意，試著使用指定的單字來完成這篇小短文。

I _____ go to an _____.
我打算要去一個藝術展。

However, the ticket price is _____ at 500 NTD.
不過，票價並不便宜，要台幣 500 元。

I don't _____ enough* _____ to buy the ticket.
我沒有足夠的錢可以買票。

I'm _____ money to buy it.
我正在存錢要買票。

I _____ I can save money _____ the art exhibition.
希望我能在藝術展之前存到錢。

Words

▶ exhibition 名詞 展覽　▶ cheap 形容詞 廉價的；便宜的

Grammar Check　　enough 足夠的；充分地

當某事物處於「充裕足夠的狀態」時，便會使用 enough 這個字，enough 可做為形容詞表達「足夠的」或副詞表示「充分地」。

1 形容詞的 enough：have enough A (名詞) to B (動詞)　有足夠的 A 去做 B
　ex) We have enough time to finish it.　我們有足夠的時間去完成它。

2 副詞的 enough：be A (形容詞) enough to B (動詞)　充分 A 而可以做 B
　ex) I am old enough to drive.　我的年紀已經大到可以開車了。

170

Step 4　自己動手寫寫看　請試著將想到的主題相關內容填進下方空格裡，然後寫出屬於你自己的文章。

Topic
Saving Money

..................., ..., ...

I plan to ....

Learn More　金額（money）的表達用語

1. 100 美元 one hundred dollars
2. 1,000 美元 one thousand dollars
3. 10,000 美元 ten thousand dollars
4. 100,000 美元 one hundred thousand dollars
5. 1,000,000 美元 one million dollars
6. 10,000,000 美元 ten million dollars

Day 34　Moving and Transferring 搬家跟轉學

Step 1　認識核心動詞

live	居住；生活	lives	lived	living
		第三人稱單數現在形	過去形	現在分詞

▪ 居住（在～）：**live＋in＋地區**

He lives in Japan.　他住在日本。

▪ （跟～）一起住：**live＋with＋對象**

I live with my aunt.　我跟我阿姨一起住。

▪ （依靠～）生活：**live＋by＋依靠的對象**

Man cannot live by bread alone.　人不能只靠麵包過活。

move	① 搬遷；移動 ② 搬動	moves	moved	moving
		第三人稱單數現在形	過去形	現在分詞

▪ 搬遷；移動：**move（to＋地點）**

Suddenly, the car moved.　突然，那台車動了。
My best friend moved to Jeju Island.　我最好的朋友搬到了濟州島。

▪ 搬動

I moved my desk to the living room.　我把我的書桌搬到了客廳。

miss	① 想念 ② 錯過	misses	missed	missing
		第三人稱單數現在形	過去形	現在分詞

▪ 想念

My mom sometimes misses my grandmother.　我媽媽有時會想念我的奶奶。

▪ 錯過

He missed the train.　他錯過了那班火車。

172

Step 2 看看別人怎麼寫
請邊聽音檔邊仔細看過一遍，接著再重新唸一遍。

住在首爾
live in Seoul

搬到釜山
move to Busan

Topic
Moving and Transferring

想念我的朋友們
miss my friends

創造很多回憶
make a lot of memories

Monday, December 29, Snowy

My family lives in Seoul.

We will move to Busan next week because of my father's job.

I also have to transfer to another school.

I'm going to miss my friends.

I will make a lot of memories with my friends before moving.

我們家住在首爾。
我們下週會因為我爸爸工作的關係而搬到釜山。
我也必須轉到另一間學校。
我會想念我的朋友們。
我會在搬家前和我的朋友們一起創造很多回憶。

Words
- because of 因為～
- job 名詞 工作
- have to 必須做～
- transfer 動詞 轉學；轉換
- memory 名詞 回憶；記憶

Step 3 依樣畫葫蘆　看一下中文語意，試著使用指定的單字來完成這篇小短文。

My family _____ Jeonju.
我們家住在全州。

We will _____ Seoul next month because of my brother's career.
我們下個月會因為我哥哥工作的關係而搬到首爾。

I also have to _____ another school.
我也必須轉到另一間學校。

I'm going to* _____.
我會想念我的朋友們。

I will* _____ with my friends before moving.
我會在搬家前和我的朋友們一起拍很多照片。

Words

▶ career 名詞（終身的）工作；職業生涯　▶ take a picture 拍照

Grammar Check　be going to vs. will 會～／將～

be going to 跟 will 都能用來描述在未來發生的事，但 will 表達的多半是「臨時或當下的決定」，be going to 表達的則是「已規劃好、預定要做的事」。舉例來說，I will help you. 指的是「當下看到對方需要幫忙，臨時決定要伸出援手」的情況，I'm going to miss my friends. 則可以解讀成「因為規劃好下週要轉學，所以現在預想自己未來會想念朋友」的情況。

174

Step 4 自己動手寫寫看
請試著將想到的主題相關內容填進下方空格裡，然後寫出屬於你自己的文章。

Topic
Moving and Transferring

.................., ..., ...

My family lives in ....

Learn More　單字小故事 ❺ trans（移動；轉變）

電影《變形金剛（Transformers）》中出現了會變換（trans）形態的機器人，字首 trans 同時具有「變換（轉變）」和「移動」之意。transfer 是「trans（移動）＋fer（攜帶）」，表示「轉移；轉學」等字義。transform 則是「trans（變換）＋form（形態）」，表示「變換；使改變」的意思。另外，translate 是「trans（移動）＋late（攜帶）」，傳達出「攜帶著語意移動（到另一種語言）」的意思，也就是字義「翻譯」的概念。

Day 35 Running 跑步

Step 1 認識核心動詞

run	跑；跑步	run**s**	r**an**	run**ning**
		第三人稱單數現在形	過去形	現在分詞

▨ 跑

He r**an** at the speed of light. 他以光速奔跑。

▨ 跑步：**run＋距離／run＋for＋時間**

I **run 1km** every day. 我每天都會跑 1 公里。
I **run for an hour** every day. 我每天都會跑 1 個小時。

fall	① 倒下，跌倒 ② 掉落	fall**s**	f**ell**	fall**ing**
		第三人稱單數現在形	過去形	現在分詞

▨ 倒下，跌倒

He twisted his foot and **fell**. 他拐到了他的腳，然後跌倒了。

▨ 掉落

The apple **fell** to the ground. 那顆蘋果掉在了地上。

> **Tip**「掉落」具有方向性，所以大多會搭配 to（往～）一起使用。

end	① 結束 ② 終止	end**s**	end**ed**	end**ing**
		第三人稱單數現在形	過去形	現在分詞

▨ 結束：**end＋in＋結果**

Her project **ended in failure**. 她的專案以失敗告終。

> **Tip** end（結束）後面加上 up（向上；完全地）的話，表示「完全結束」，也就是「以～告終／作收」的意思。

▨ 終止

When the bell rang, the teacher **ended** class. 老師在鐘聲響的時候下課了。

176

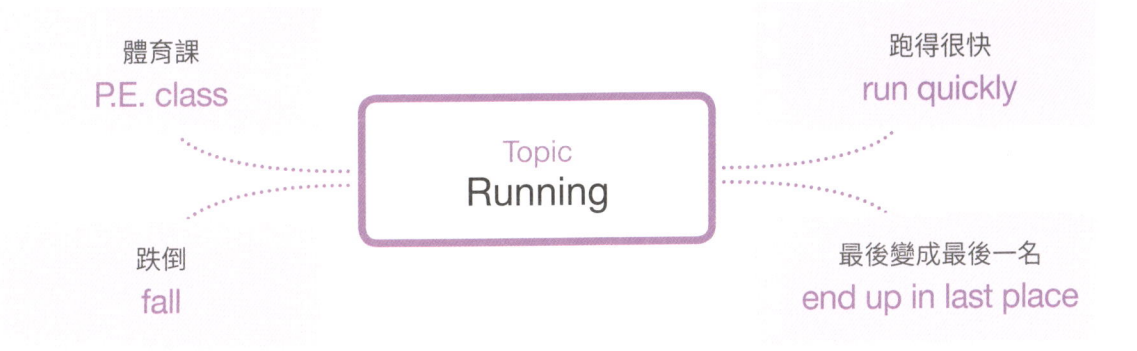

Step 2 看看別人怎麼寫
請邊聽音檔邊仔細看過一遍，接著再重新唸一遍。

體育課　P.E. class
跑得很快　run quickly
跌倒　fall
最後變成最後一名　end up in last place

Topic: Running

Friday, October 20, Cool

Our class ran during P.E. class.

I ran quickly at the start signal.

I was running first.

Suddenly, my shoelaces were untied.

I fell and ended up in last place.

我們班在體育課的時候跑步。
我一聽到起跑信號就衝了。
那時我跑第一名。
突然，我的鞋帶鬆開了。
我跌倒了，結果最後變成最後一名。

Words

- during 介系詞 在～期間
- at the start signal 一聽到起跑信號就～
- suddenly 副詞 突然地
- shoelace 名詞 鞋帶
- untied 形容詞 鬆開的；解開的
- place 名詞 （競賽的）排名，名次

Step 3 依樣畫葫蘆　看一下中文語意，試著使用指定的單字來完成這篇小短文。

Our class _____ during* P.E. class.
我們班在體育課的時候跑步。

I ran quickly at the sound of _____.
哨聲一響我就衝了。

I was running _____.
那時我跑第二名。

Suddenly, I _____ the friend next to me.
突然，我撞到了在我旁邊的朋友。

I _____ and _____ in last place.
我跌倒了，結果最後變成最後一名。

Words

▸ whistle 名詞 哨聲　▸ bump (into) 動詞 撞到～

Grammar Check　during 在～的期間

during 描述的是「（從開始到結束的）一段期間」，當在那段期間內發生了什麼事，就可以使用 during 這個字。上方短文裡提到的 during P.E. class 也可以翻成「在體育課期間」或「在上體育課的時候」發生了某件事（這裡是「跑步」），所以只要一看到 during 這個字，就可以知道在那段期間裡一定有發生了某件事。

ex) I studied English during vacation.　我在放假的時候念了英文。
　　　　發生的事　　　　期間

Step 4 自己動手寫寫看　請試著將想到的主題相關內容填進下方空格裡，然後寫出屬於你自己的文章。

Topic
Running

Learn More　跟 run 有關的表達用語

1. run away from 逃離～
2. run away to 逃到～
3. run out of ～用完，耗盡～　ex) I ran out of money. 我把錢用完了。
4. run into 跑進～；與～偶然遇到

179

Review Test 7　(Day 31~35)

A　請寫出與以下中文相對應的英文動詞。

1. 哭泣；喊叫 → cry
2. 居住；生活 → l
3. 清洗；洗澡；洗衣服 → w
4. 跑；跑步 → r
5. 計劃，打算（做某件事）；制定計畫，規劃 → p
6. 解決；解答 → s
7. 理解，懂得 → u
8. 結束；終止 → e
9. 想念；錯過 → m
10. 打破，打碎；弄壞；破損；壞掉，故障 → b
11. 搬遷，移動；搬動 → m
12. 存～；拯救，挽救 → s
13. 說 → s
14. 希望 → h
15. 倒下，跌倒；掉落 → f

B　請將英文單字與相對應的中文意思連起來。

1. job
2. content
3. suddenly
4. startled
5. untied
6. decide
7. miss
8. expensive
9. careful
10. transfer

ⓐ 內容
ⓑ 吃驚的，嚇一跳的
ⓒ 想念；錯過
ⓓ 工作
ⓔ 突然地
ⓕ 鬆開的；解開的
ⓖ 小心的
ⓗ 轉學；轉換
ⓘ 昂貴的
ⓙ 決定

C 請根據中文句意將適當的字詞填入空格之中，完成英文句子。

1. Mom told me to _____be careful_____ next time.
   媽媽叫我下次要小心一點。

2. I decided to _____ for 30 minutes every day.
   我決定每天複習課程內容 30 分鐘。

3. I don't have _____ to buy the ticket.
   我沒有足夠的錢買票。

4. I also have to _____ another school.
   我也必須轉到另一間學校。

5. I _____ at the sound of a whistle.
   哨聲一響我就衝了。

D 請利用下列提示的英文動詞來寫出符合中文句意的英文句子。

1. wash — I was washing the dishes.
   我那時正在洗碗。

2. come, cry _____
   我回到家哭了。

3. save _____
   我正在存錢要買那個票。

4. live _____
   我們家住在首爾。

5. fall, end _____
   我跌倒了，結果最後變成最後一名。

Week 8

Day 36 **choose, enter, know** ▸ 科博館

Day 37 **hate, lie** ▸ 說謊

Day 38 **find, clean, remember** ▸ 找皮夾

Day 39 **have, swim, speak** ▸ 朋友的優點

Day 40 **draw, show, hang** ▸ 稱讚

Review Test 8

Day 36　Science Museum 科博館

Step 1　認識核心動詞

| choose | ① 選擇
② 選取 | chooses
第三人稱單數現在形 | chose
過去形 | choosing
現在分詞 |

▨ 選擇：**choose＋A＋from/among/between/out of＋B**

　You have to choose one out of seven. 你必須從七個裡選一個。

▨ 選取（A 做為 B）：**choose＋A＋as＋B**

　We chose him as the class leader. 我們選了他當班長。

| enter | ① 進入；進去
② 入學；參加 | enters
第三人稱單數現在形 | entered
過去形 | entering
現在分詞 |

▨ 進入；進去

　He entered the room. 他進入了那個房間。
　Tip enter 也有「輸入（資料）」的意思，電腦鍵盤上甚至還有一個 [Enter] 鍵。

▨ 入學；參加

　I will enter middle school next year. 我明年會進入國中。
　Tip graduate (from)：（從～）畢業
　　He *graduated from* elementary school. 他從小學畢業了。

| know | 知道；了解 | knows
第三人稱單數現在形 | knew
過去形 | knowing
現在分詞 |

▨ 知道

　Do you know him? 你認識他嗎？

▨ 了解～：**know＋about＋內容**

　He wants to know about various cultures. 他想要了解各式各樣的文化。

Step 2　看看別人怎麼寫　請邊聽音檔邊仔細看過一遍，接著再重新唸一遍。

去科博館
go to the science museum

選擇看 3D 電影
choose watching a 3D movie

Topic
Science Museum

忘記時間
lose track of time

開始對科學產生興趣
become interested in science

Wednesday, September 22, Clear

Our class went to the science museum.

I **chose** watching a 3D movie among the activities.

I **entered** the theater and put on the 3D glasses.

The movie was so fun that I lost track of time.

I didn't **know** much **about** science, but today I became interested in it.

我們班去了科博館。
我在各種活動之中選了去看 3D 電影。
我進到電影院裡並戴上了 3D 眼鏡。
那部電影有趣到讓我忘了時間。
我對科學不太了解，不過我今天開始對它產生興趣了。

Words

- museum 名詞 博物館
- among 介系詞 在～之中
- activity 名詞 活動
- put on 穿／戴上
- lose track of 忘記～；失去～的連繫
- interested 形容詞 感興趣的

Step 3 依樣畫葫蘆 看一下中文語意，試著使用指定的單字來完成這篇小短文。

Our class went to _____.
我們班去了科博館。

I _____ observation of constellations _____ the activities.
我在各種活動之中選了觀星。

I _____ the observation room.
我進到了觀測室裡。

The observation was so* _____ that* I lost track of time.
這次觀星令人興奮到忘了時間。

I didn't _____ much _____, but today I became _____ in it.
我對宇宙不太了解，不過我今天開始對它產生興趣了。

Words

- **observation** 名詞 觀測；觀察
- **constellation** 名詞 星座
- **exciting** 形容詞 令人興奮的
- **universe** 名詞 宇宙

Grammar Check　so ~ that ~ 非常～以致於～

這個慣用表達的句型架構是「主詞＋動詞＋so＋A（形容詞，表「原因」）＋that＋B（主詞＋動詞，表「結果」）」，意思是「主詞非常地 A，以致於發生了 B」。透過例句來看看這個句型吧！在 I was so tired that I went to bed early. 這一句中，I was tired（我很累）是原因，而 I went to bed early.（我很早就睡了）則是結果。英文裡有個有趣的慣用表達，用的就是這個句型，一起記下來吧！

ex) I'm **so** hungry **that** I could eat a horse. 我餓到可以吃下一匹馬。

186

Step 4　自己動手寫寫看　請試著將想到的主題相關內容填進下方空格裡，然後寫出屬於你自己的文章。

Topic
Science Museum

..................., ...,

Our class went to the science museum. ....

Learn More　3D movie（3D 電影）

英文縮寫 3D 裡的 D，指的是 dimensional（次元的）的意思。1 次元指的是「線」，2 次元指的是「平面」，一般我們看的電影即是 2D。3D 指的則是「立體（空間）」，在戴上 3D 眼鏡看電影時，就會覺得電影裡的角色似乎真的正在朝著你走來，這種電影就叫做 3D 電影。除 3D 電影外，最近也出現了 4D 電影，4D 電影就是在播放過程中，加入了能夠刺激「感官」的元素，例如風、水或氣味等來提升觀影體驗。

Day 37　Lie 說謊

Step 1　認識核心動詞

hate	討厭	hates	hated	hating
		第三人稱單數現在形	過去形	現在分詞

▨ 討厭
I hate violence.　我討厭暴力。

▨ 討厭（做～）：**hate＋to＋動詞／hate＋V-ing**
He hates to wash. / He hates washing.　他討厭洗澡。

lie	說謊	lies	lied	lying
		第三人稱單數現在形	過去形	現在分詞

▨ （對～）說謊：**lie＋to＋對象**
She lied to me.　她對我說了謊。
　Tip　lie 也可做為名詞，表示「謊言」。

▨ 對～說謊：**lie＋about＋內容**
He lied about stealing the wallet.　他對偷皮夾的這件事說了謊。
　Tip　lie 有同字異義的兩種形態，下方的 lie（躺；呈現（某種狀態））無論是語意還是過去形的拼字方式，都與表示「說謊」的 lie 截然不同，因此是只有動詞基本形相同的兩個完全不同的單字。

lie	① 躺 ② 呈現（某種狀態）	lies	lay	lying
		第三人稱單數現在形	過去形	現在分詞

▨ 躺：**lie (down)**
I lay down on the floor and soon fell asleep.
我躺在了地板上，很快就睡著了。

▨ 呈現（某種狀態）
The flowers lie wilted in the sun.　這些花在陽光下呈現出枯萎的樣子。

188

Step 2 看看別人怎麼寫
請邊聽音檔邊仔細看過一遍，接著再重新唸一遍。

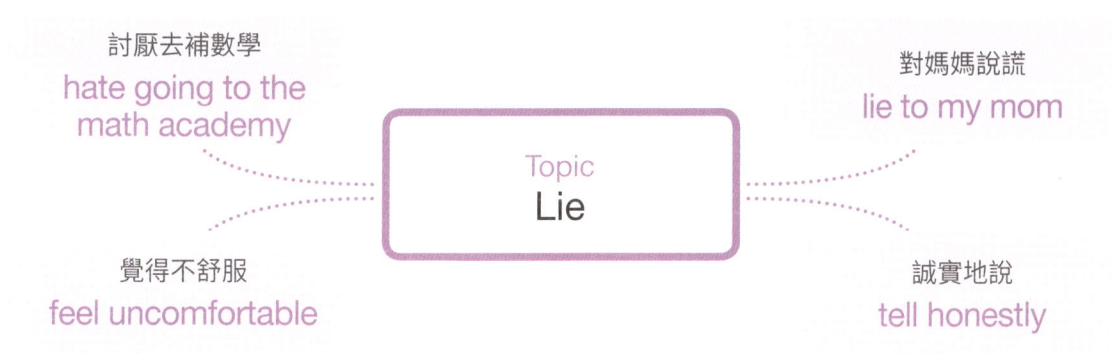

討厭去補數學
hate going to the math academy

對媽媽說謊
lie to my mom

Topic
Lie

覺得不舒服
feel uncomfortable

誠實地說
tell honestly

Thursday, July 28, Hot

I hated going to the math academy. I lied to my mom,

"I have a stomachache."

She said to me, "If you have a severe stomachache,

don't go to the academy."

I thought it would feel good lying on the bed all day.

However, I felt uncomfortable because I lied.

I told her honestly and went to the academy.

我討厭去補數學。我對媽媽說謊說：「我肚子痛。」
她對我說：「如果你肚子痛得厲害，那就不要去補習班了。」
我以為躺在床上一整天會覺得很開心。
可是，我覺得很不舒服，因為我說謊了。
我跟她說了實話，然後就去補習了。

Words
- **academy** 名詞 （專項）補習班
- **stomachache** 名詞 肚子痛，胃痛
- **if** 連接詞 如果～的話
- **severe** 形容詞 嚴重的
- **think** 動詞 認為 *過去形 thought
- **uncomfortable** 形容詞 不舒服的
- **honestly** 副詞 誠實地，坦白地

Step 3 依樣畫葫蘆　看一下中文語意，試著使用指定的單字來完成這篇小短文。

I _____ to the _____ academy.
我討厭去補英文。

I _____ my mom, "I have _____."
我對媽媽說謊說：「我頭痛。」

She said to me, "If* you have _____, don't go to the academy."
她對我說：「如果你頭痛得厲害，那就不要去補習班了。」

I _____ it would _____ lying on the bed all day.
我以為躺在床上一整天會覺得很開心。

However, I felt _____ because I lied.
可是，我覺得很不舒服，因為我說謊了。

I told her _____ and went to the academy.
我跟她說了實話，然後就去補習了。

Words

▶ headache 名詞 頭痛　▶ truth 名詞 真相

Grammar Check　　if 如果～的話

if 描述的是某個「不確定未來會不會發生」的事情。在上方的短文裡，媽媽因為無法確定孩子的頭到底有多痛，而使用了 if 來表達兩種「可能性」，也就是「頭痛不嚴重 → 去補習」和「頭痛很嚴重 → 不去補習」。

ex) **If** you get 100 in math, I'll buy you a smart phone.
　　如果你的數學考 100 分，我會買一支智慧型手機給你。

Step 4　自己動手寫寫看　請試著將想到的主題相關內容填進下方空格裡，然後寫出屬於你自己的文章。

Topic
Lie

..................., ..., ...

I lied to ....

Learn More　跟「說謊」有關的俗語

1. One lie makes many.　撒了一個謊，就得用更多謊來圓。
2. A liar should have a good memory.　騙子得有好記性。
3. You have cried wolf too many times.　你已經「狼來了」太多次了。
（你已經說謊說太多次了。）

Day 38　Finding the Wallet 找皮夾

Step 1　認識核心動詞

find	① 找到；發現 ② 意識到；發覺	find**s**	f**ound**	find**ing**
		第三人稱單數現在形	過去形	現在分詞

◾ 找到；發現

　　She **found** a secret space.　她發現了一個祕密空間。

◾ 意識到；發覺：**find (out)＋that＋主詞＋動詞**

　　I **found (out) that I had made** a mistake.　我發覺我犯了一個錯。

　Tip find 的過去形 found 跟字義是「建立，創立」的動詞 found 一模一樣。found 的過去形是 founded。

　　My uncle *founded* a company.　我叔叔創立了一間公司。

clean	打掃；清潔	clean**s**	clean**ed**	clean**ing**
		第三人稱單數現在形	過去形	現在分詞

◾ 打掃；清潔：**clean (up)**

　　I **cleaned (up)** the living room after lunch.　我在午餐後打掃了客廳。

　Tip clean 經常做為形容詞使用，表示「乾淨的」。

　　His room was *clean*.　他的房間很乾淨。

remember	記得，想起	remember**s**	remember**ed**	remember**ing**
		第三人稱單數現在形	過去形	現在分詞

◾ 記得

　　Do you **remember** his name?　你記得他的名字嗎？

◾ 想起，記得（做過～）：**remember＋V-ing**

　　He didn't **remember going** there.　他不記得去過那裡。

192

Step 2 看看別人怎麼寫
請邊聽音檔邊仔細看過一遍，接著再重新唸一遍。

試圖找到我的皮夾
try to find my wallet

我的房間很亂
my room is messy

Topic
Finding the Wallet

打掃
clean up

把它放到我的夾克裡
put it inside my jacket

Tuesday, August 5, Hot

I need money to buy ice cream.

So I tried to find my wallet in my room.

However, my room was very messy.

I cleaned up my room first. I still couldn't find my wallet.

Suddenly, I remembered putting it inside my jacket.

我需要錢來買冰淇淋。
所以我試圖要在房間裡找到我的皮夾。
可是，我的房間非常亂。
我先打掃了我的房間。
我還是找不到我的皮夾。
突然，我想起我把它放到我的夾克裡了。

Words

▶ wallet 名詞 皮夾　▶ messy 形容詞 凌亂的　▶ still 副詞 仍然，還是　▶ inside 介系詞 在～的裡面

193

Step 3 依樣畫葫蘆　看一下中文語意，試著使用指定的單字來完成這篇小短文。

I need a _____ card to go to my friend's house.

我需要一張交通卡來去我朋友家。

So I tried to _____ in my room.

所以我試圖要在我的房間裡找到那張交通卡。

However, my room was not _____.

可是，我的房間不太整齊。

I _____ my room first. I _____ find the card.

我先打掃了我的房間。我還是找不到那張交通卡。

Suddenly, I _____ it inside my bag.

突然，我想起我把它放到我的包包裡了。

Words

▶ **transportation** 名詞 交通工具；運輸　▶ **tidy** 形容詞 整齊的，整潔的

Grammar Check　　still 仍然，還是

如果你對其他人說：「還沒嗎？」，那就表示「某件事花費的時間比你原本預期的要更久」，這種時候就可以用 still 來表達。still 可以用在肯定句，例如 He is still there.（他還在那裡），若要在否定句中使用，則 still 要放在否定詞之前。

ex) He **still doesn't** know the answer. 他仍然不知道答案。

Step 4　自己動手寫寫看　請試著將想到的主題相關內容填進下方空格裡，然後寫出屬於你自己的文章。

Topic
Finding _____

..................., ...,

I need _____

So I tried to find _____

Learn More　描述位置的表達用語

- **inside** 在（較小的範圍或地點）的裡面　ex) inside the pocket 在口袋裡面
- **under** 在～的（正）下方　ex) under the table 在桌子下方
- **above** 在～的上方　ex) There is a bird above your head. 在你頭的上方有一隻鳥。
- **behind** 在～的後方　ex) The supermarket is behind this building. 這間超市在這棟大樓的後方。
- **next to** 在～的旁邊　ex) The police station is next to the post office. 警局在郵局旁邊。

195

Day 39 Strengths of My Friend 朋友的優點

Step 1 認識核心動詞

have	① 擁有（身體或心理上的特質） ② 吃；喝	has	had	having
		第三人稱單數現在形	過去形	現在分詞

1 分鐘小教室

在 Day 13 中曾學過 have 的基本字義是「有」，藉此可衍生出其他語意，如「擁有（身體或心理上的特質）」和「吃；喝」等字義。

▨ 擁有（身體或心理上的特質）

He has a habit of nail-biting. 他有咬指甲的習慣。

▨ 吃；喝

We had dinner together.
我們一起吃了晚餐。

swim	游泳	swims	swam	swimming
		第三人稱單數現在形	過去形	現在分詞

▨ 游泳

Can you swim? 你會游泳嗎？

▨ 去游泳：**go swimming** ＊請參考 Day 8

Do you want to go swimming tomorrow? 你明天想要去游泳嗎？

Tip 游泳是「在水裡面」的狀態，因此後面大多會用 in 來接地點，表示在某地點裡游泳的意思。
　　 swim in the sea 在海中游泳　　swim in the pool 在游泳池裡游泳

speak	說	speaks	spoke	speaking
		第三人稱單數現在形	過去形	現在分詞

▨ 說

Can you speak Korean? 你會說韓文嗎？

▨ （用～）說：**speak＋in**

He spoke in a quiet voice. 他低聲說了話。

▨ 對～說～：**speak＋to＋對象＋about＋主題**

She spoke to me about her vacation plans. 她對我說了她的度假計畫。

Step 2 看看別人怎麼寫 請邊聽音檔邊仔細看過一遍，接著再重新唸一遍。

MP3-039

我最好的朋友 Min-su
my best friend Min-su

非常會游泳
swim very well

Topic
Strengths of My Friend

說英文和中文
speak English and Chinese

很會幫忙朋友
help friends well

Saturday, January 3, Cold

My best friend Min-su **has** many strengths.

He **swims** very well.

He can **speak** English and Chinese.

He also helps his friends well.

I will try hard to become a wonderful student like Min-su.

我最好的朋友 Min-su 有很多優點。
他非常會游泳。
他會說英文和中文。
他還很會幫朋友的忙。
我會努力成為像 Min-su 一樣棒的學生。

Words

- strength 名詞 優點；力量
- well 副詞 很好地；充分地

Step 3　依樣畫葫蘆　看一下中文語意，試著使用指定的單字來完成這篇小短文。

My best friend Woo-bin _____.
我最好的朋友 Woo-bin 有很多優點。

He _____ very well.
他非常會游泳。

He can _____ and _____.
他會說日語和西班牙語。

He also _____ well.
他跳繩也跳得很好。

I will try hard to _____ like* Woo-bin.
我會努力成為像 Woo-bin 一樣棒的學生。

Words

▸ Japanese 名詞 日語　▸ Spanish 名詞 西班牙語　▸ jump rope 跳繩
▸ great 形容詞 偉大的；優秀的

Grammar Check　　like 跟～一樣，像～一般

看到 like 這個字，首先會想到的字義是「喜歡」，但 like 也能做為介系詞，表示「跟～一樣，像～一般」。一起透過下面的例句來了解要怎麼使用 like 吧！

ex) She ran like the wind. 她跑得像風一樣快。
　　Her face turned red like an apple. 她的臉變得像蘋果一樣紅。

Step 4 自己動手寫寫看　請試著將想到的主題相關內容填進下方空格裡，然後寫出屬於你自己的文章。

Topic: Strengths of My Friend

_____, _____, _____

My best friend _____ has many strengths.

Learn More　國家／語言／人

	韓國	日本	中國	美國	西班牙
國家	Korea	Japan	China	America	Spain
語言	Korean	Japanese	Chinese	American English	Spanish
人	Korean	Japanese	Chinese	American	Spaniard

199

Day 40　Praise 稱讚

Step 1　認識核心動詞

draw	① 劃（線）；畫（圖） ② 拖；拉 ③ （在比賽中）打成平手	draws	drew	drawing
		第三人稱單數現在形	過去形	現在分詞

▨ 劃（線）；畫（圖）
The children drew some pictures with colored pencils. 這些孩子們用色鉛筆畫了一些圖。

▨ 拖；拉
He drew the chair in front of the desk. 他把椅子拖到了書桌的前面。

▨ （在比賽中）打成平手：**draw＋with＋對象**
Korea played soccer and drew with China. 韓國和中國在足球比賽中踢成了平手。

show	顯現；給～看	shows	showed	showing
		第三人稱單數現在形	過去形	現在分詞

▨ 顯現；給～看：**show＋對象＋物品／show＋物品＋to＋對象**
I showed her a book. / I showed a book to her.
我給她看了一本書。／我拿了一本書給她看。
　Tip show 也常做為名詞使用，表示「表演；節目」。
　　a TV quiz show 電視問答節目

hang	① 懸掛；吊起 ② 掛著，吊著	hangs	hung	hanging
		第三人稱單數現在形	過去形	現在分詞

▨ 懸掛；吊起
He hung a picture frame on the wall. 他在牆上掛了一個畫框。

▨ 掛著，吊著
There is a clock hanging on the wall. 牆上掛著一個時鐘。

Step 2 看看別人怎麼寫
請邊聽音檔邊仔細看過一遍，接著再重新唸一遍。

在美術課上畫畫
draw in art class

把我的畫給老師看
show my picture to the teacher

Topic
Praise

她稱讚我
she praises me

覺得很有自信
feel confident

Monday, April 19, Sunny

I **drew** in art class today. I **showed** my picture **to** the teacher.

She patted my shoulder and praised me.

I **hung** my picture at the back of the classroom.

My classmates envied me when they saw my picture.

I felt confident in drawing.

今天我在美術課上畫了畫。我把我的畫給老師看。
她輕拍了我的肩膀並稱讚我。
我把我的畫掛在了教室後面。
我的同學們在看到了我的畫時都很羨慕我。
我對畫畫覺得很有自信。

Words

- **pat** 動詞 輕拍，輕打
- **shoulder** 名詞 肩膀
- **praise** 動詞 稱讚 名詞 讚美
- **envy** 動詞 忌妒；羨慕

Step 3 依樣畫葫蘆 看一下中文語意，試著使用指定的單字來完成這篇小短文。

I _____ in art class today.
今天我在美術課上畫了畫。

I _____ my picture _____ the teacher.
我把我的畫給老師看。

She _____ and praised me.
她笑容燦爛地稱讚了我。

I _____ my picture _____* the classroom.
我把我的畫掛在了教室後面。

My classmates _____ me _____ they saw my picture.
我的同學們在看到了我的畫時都很羨慕我。

I _____ in drawing.
我對畫畫有了信心。

Words

▸ smile 動詞 微笑　▸ brightly 副詞 燦爛地，明亮地　▸ gain 動詞 得到，獲得
▸ confidence 名詞 自信，信心

Grammar Check　at 在～

at 的基本概念是「（時間或空間中的）一個點」。在上方短文裡，因為說話者的畫是掛在教室後方的牆面上（也就是空間中的一個位置點），所以使用 at 來表達。at 大多會翻成「在～」，但請記得 at 的正確基本概念應該是「（時間或空間中的）一個點」才對。

ex) I get up at 6. （時間）我在 6 點起床。
　　We met at the bank. （空間）我們在銀行見了面。

Step 4 自己動手寫寫看
請試著將想到的主題相關內容填進下方空格裡，然後寫出屬於你自己的文章。

Topic
Praise

Learn More　跟「繪畫／圖畫」有關的表達用語

1. **draw**（沒有著色，用鉛筆或鋼筆等等）畫
   ex) He drew a triangle.
   他畫了一個三角形。
2. **paint**（用顏料）畫
3. **sketch** 速寫，素描；打草稿
4. **color** 著色
   ex) I colored the apples red.
   我把這些蘋果塗成了紅色。

1. **portrait** 肖像畫 *以人像為主題的畫
2. **self-portrait** 自畫像 *自己畫自己的肖像畫
3. **landscape** 風景畫 描繪大自然景色的畫
4. **still life** 靜物畫 *描繪靜止物體的畫
5. **watercolor** 水彩畫
   *將顏料用水調和後使用所繪製的畫

203

Review Test 8 (Day 36~40)

A 請根據中文正確排列英文字母並將相對應的英文動詞填入框中。

#	中文	字母	答案
1	知道；了解	wonk	know
2	打掃；清潔	aelnc	
3	躺；呈現（某種狀態）	eil	
4	討厭	etah	
5	擁有（身體或心理上的特質）；吃；喝	ahev	
6	選擇；選取	eshooc	
7	劃（線）；畫（圖）；拖；拉；（在比賽中）打成平手	ward	
8	找到；發現；意識到；發覺	dnfi	
9	說	sekpa	
10	進入；進去；入學；參加	etnre	
11	記得；想起	eeebrrmm	
12	游泳	iwsm	
13	說謊	iel	
14	懸掛；吊起；掛著，吊著	nahg	
15	顯現；給～看	hwso	

B 請找到跟中文相對應的英文單字並標示出來，然後將單字填入空格之中。

```
d e q r a y w v c q
v m d e c m e s s y
y o c d t e o e h q
d c f l i d c n t q
n e s u v a w v g i
o b e o i c i y n w
w z v h t a y o e a
e l e s y e m d r q
k o r p i z i x t w
b t e l l a w p s t
```

#	中文	答案
1	活動	activity
2	在～之中	a_____
3	（專項）補習班	a_____
4	嚴重的	s_____
5	皮夾	w_____
6	凌亂的	m_____
7	優點；力量	s_____
8	成為～	b_____
9	肩膀	s_____
10	忌妒；羨慕	e_____

C 請根據中文句意將適當的字詞填入空格之中，完成英文句子。

1. Our class went to ___the science museum___.
   我們班去了科博館。

2. I felt _____ because I lied.
   我覺得不舒服，因為我說了謊。

3. I _____ find the card.
   我還是找不到那張卡。

4. He also _____ well.
   他跳繩也跳得很好。

5. She _____ and praised me.
   她笑容燦爛地稱讚了我。

D 請利用下列提示的英文字詞來寫出符合中文句意的英文句子。

1. ___I entered the theater and put on the 3D glasses.___
   我進了電影院並戴上 3D 眼鏡。　(3D glasses / I / the / entered / and / the / put / theater / on)

2. _____
   我討厭去補數學。　　　　　　　(academy / to / I / the / hated / math / going)

3. _____
   我試圖要在房間裡找到我的皮夾。　(find / to / I / my / tried / room / wallet / my / in)

4. _____
   我最好的朋友 Min-su 有很多優點。　(strengths / best / My / Min-su / many / has / friend)

5. _____
   我把我的畫給老師看。　　　　　　(to / I / teacher / the / picture / my / showed)

205

解 答

Week 1

Day 1 Volunteer Day
志工日 p.18

Today was a volunteer day.
I went to the playground with my teacher.
We picked up the trash and put it in the trash can.
It was rewarding.
I was refreshed because the playground was clean.

Day 2 P.E. Class
體育課 p.22

I played basketball with my friends in P.E. class.
I scored 2 goals in the first half.
It was a close game, but my team won.
I shouted with joy.
Hard work pays off.

Day 3 Oversleep
睡過頭 p.26

I woke up late in the morning.
I didn't hear the alarm.
I hurried to school without washing my face.
I arrived at school after the second period.
I quietly entered the classroom through the front door.

Day 4 Watching Movies
看電影 p.30

I watched the movie Spider-Man with my sister.
I ate potato chips while watching the movie.
The movie was tense.
Two and a half hours passed quickly.
I will introduce the movie to my friends tomorrow.

Day 5 Visiting Grandmother
探望奶奶 p.34

I visit my grandmother every month.
Last month, she baked a pie.
It smelled really good.
I ate a piece of pie, and it tasted sweet.
My grandmother smiled happily.

Review Test 1 .... pp.36~37

A 1 visit 2 hurry 3 score 4 go 5 smell
6 watch 7 wake 8 play 9 introduce
10 pick 11 win 12 arrive 13 bake

B 1 ⓒ 2 ⓓ 3 ⓗ 4 ⓐ 5 ⓘ
6 ⓑ 7 ⓙ 8 ⓕ 9 ⓔ 10 ⓖ

C 1 picked up the trash, trash can
2 scored, first half
3 woke up, morning
4 Two and a half hours
5 a piece of, sweet

D 1 I went to the park with my classmates.
2 I played soccer with my friends in P.E. class.
3 I hurried to school without eating breakfast.
4 I will introduce the movie to my friends tomorrow.
5 I visit my grandmother every week.

Week 2

Day 6 Birthday Party
生日派對 p.42

Today was my 11th birthday.
I invited friends to my birthday party.
They came to my house 30 minutes late.
They prepared a present for my birthday.
I opened it. It was a nice pencil case.
I was satisfied with it.

Day 7 Meeting Friends
遇到朋友 p.46

On my way to the academy, I met Min-su on the street.
Min-su looked in a bad mood.
I asked him, "How are you?"
He said, "I failed the Korean history exam."
I comforted him.

Day 8 Going Skating
去溜冰 p.50

I went skating with my family.
It was my second time skating.
The ice floor was hard.
I held my father's hand.
I moved forward confidently.
I was excited and sweated a little.

Day 9 Buying a Hat
買帽子 p.54

As winter came, the wind became cold.
I needed a scarf.
My mother bought it online three days ago.
It was delivered today.
However, I didn't like the scarf so I will change it.

Day 10 Climbing
爬山 p.58

I climbed Mt. Halla.
The weather was warm for climbing.
Various trees were growing on the mountain.
The sky view from the top was really wonderful.
I drank cool orange juice at the summit.

Review Test 2 .... pp.60~61

A 1 invite 2 come 3 open 4 meet 5 ask
   6 fail 7 go skating 8 hold 9 need 10 buy
   11 change 12 climb 13 grow 14 drink

B 1 wallet 2 prepare 3 street 4 mood
   5 nervous 6 sweat 7 become 8 deliver
   9 mountain 10 weather

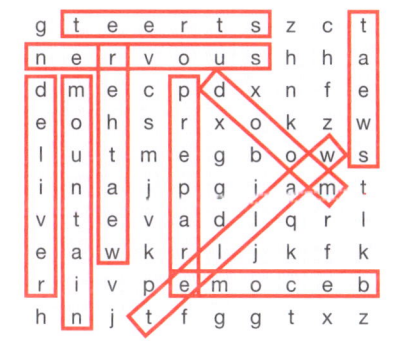

g	t	e	e	r	t	s	z	c	t
n	e	r	v	o	u	s	h	h	a
d	m	e	c	p	d	x	n	f	e
e	o	h	r	x	o	k	z	w	w
l	u	t	m	e	g	b	o	w	s
i	n	a	j	p	g	i	a	m	t
v	t	e	v	a	d	l	r	l	l
e	a	w	k	r	l	j	k	f	k
r	i	v	p	e	m	o	c	e	b
h	n	j	t	f	g	g	t	x	z

C 1 prepared
   2 failed, Korean history
   3 confidently
   4 winter, cold
   5 warm

D 1 I invited friends to my birthday party.
   2 I met Min-su on the street.
   3 I went skating with my family.
   4 My mother bought a hat online two days ago.
   5 Many plants were growing on the mountain.

Week 3

Day 11 — School Festival
校慶 p.66

Yesterday was our school festival day.
There were a lot of events.
I danced to K-pop music.
Jane sang 'Perfect' by Ed Sheeran.
Many of my friends cheered.
My friend recorded my dancing, then I watched the video clip.

Day 12 — Borrowing Books
借書 p.70

I needed a book to do my social studies homework.
I borrowed 3 books from the local library.
The rental period for those books was 2 weeks.
But I forgot to return them.
I can't borrow books for a week.

Day 13 — Bad Cold
重感冒 p.74

I had a bad cold. I went to the pharmacy.
There were many patients in the pharmacy.
I waited for 30 minutes.
The pharmacist gave me medicine.
I took medicine and took a nap.

Day 14 — Catching Dragonflies
抓蜻蜓 p.78

Butterflies were flying around the garden.
I tried to catch them.
However, it was difficult.
I waited until the butterflies sat on the leaves and stopped.
In the end, I caught one.

Day 15 — King Sejong
世宗大王 p.82

I read the biography of King Gwanggaeto.
He was the nineteenth king of Goguryeo.
He loved his people very much.
He expanded the country.
He died in 412.

Review Test 3 .... pp.84~85

A 1 have 2 fly 3 dance 4 forget 5 take
6 die 7 borrow 8 wait 9 try 10 sing
11 return 12 record 13 catch 14 love 15 read

B 1 ⓑ 2 ⓓ 3 ⓔ 4 ⓐ 5 ⓒ
6 ⓖ 7 ⓕ 8 ⓙ 9 ⓘ 10 ⓗ

C 1 a lot of
2 The rental period
3 The pharmacist
4 In the end
5 expanded

D 1 I danced to K-pop music.
2 I borrowed 3 books from the library.
3 I waited for 30 minutes.
4 I tried to catch dragonflies.
5 He loved his people very much.

Week 4

Day 16 Sending a Message

傳訊息 ·· p.90

I'm not good at English.

I asked Sharon for help.

Sharon helped me write English.

I sent her a message at night, "Thank you for helping me."

Sharon sent a reply soon, "I was glad to help you."

Day 17 Flea Market

跳蚤市場 ·· p.94

There will be a flea market at the apartment complex tomorrow.

I thought about what to take.

There are a lot of dolls in my room.

I will sell some of them tomorrow.

I'm looking forward to tomorrow.

Day 18 Exercise

運動 ·· p.98

Adults say health is the most important thing.

Today, the school health teacher said, "We should exercise three days a week."

I don't like exercising; I like watching TV.

I need to exercise for my health.

I will start walking every other day from tomorrow.

Day 19 Discussing Middle School Entrance

討論國中入學的事 ·· p.102

I will become a middle school student next year.

I discussed middle school entrance with my mom.

I wanted to go to an art middle school.

However, she wanted me to go to a nearby school.

I talked to her for one hour, and she agreed with my decision.

Day 20 Learning Guitar

學吉他 ·· p.106

My older sister is good at playing the piano.

I learned to play the piano from her.

My arms hurt when I played the piano.

However, I feel better when I play the piano.

I will practice the piano every day.

I believe in myself.

Review Test 4 ·· pp.108~109

A ① sell ② become ③ walk ④ learn ⑤ help ⑥ believe ⑦ agree ⑧ exercise ⑨ send ⑩ start ⑪ discuss ⑫ think ⑬ practice

B ① solve ② problem ③ flea ④ apartment ⑤ should ⑥ important ⑦ entrance ⑧ nearby ⑨ better ⑩ myself

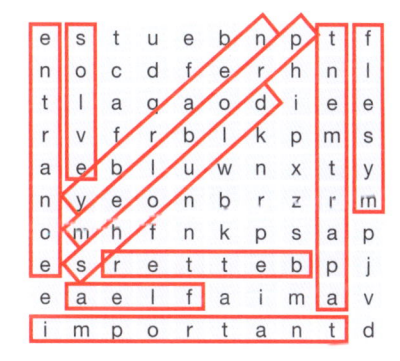

e	s	t	u	e	b	n	p	t	f
n	o	c	d	f	e	r	h	n	l
t	l	a	g	a	o	d	i	e	e
r	v	f	r	b	l	k	p	m	s
a	e	b	l	u	w	n	x	t	y
n	y	e	o	n	b	r	z	r	m
o	m	h	f	n	k	p	s	a	
e	s	r	e	t	t	e	b	p	j
	e	a	e	l	f	a	i	m	a
	i	m	p	o	r	t	a	n	t	d

C ① good at English
   ② looking forward to
   ③ Adults, important thing
   ④ art middle school
   ⑤ My arms

D ① John helped me solve a math problem.
   ② I thought about what to take.
   ③ I will start walking every day from tomorrow.
   ④ I discussed middle school entrance with my mom.
   ⑤ I will practice the guitar every day.

211

Week 5

Day 21 Boring Day
無聊的日子 p.114

I felt bored all day.

I called Kevin but he didn't have time to talk with me.

I tried talking to my younger brother.

However, he was busy with his homework.

In the end, I spent my time tidying up my room.

Day 22 My Hobby
我的嗜好 p.118

My hobby is collecting favorite singer's albums.

I have over thirty albums.

I listen to album music almost every day.

I sometimes turn on the smart TV and watch music videos.

I try easy dances while watching the music video.

Day 23 Broken Bike
壞掉的腳踏車 p.122

I hit the wall while carrying the bookshelf, and it broke.

My dad fixed and painted my bookshelf today.

I helped him paint.

It took 2 hours to finish the work.

After all, I stayed at home and helped my dad all afternoon.

Day 24 Congratulations!
恭喜！ p.126

I went to see my friend's violin recital today.

She played the violin really well.

After the recital, I congratulated her.

I gave a sunflower to her.

She thanked me.

Day 25 Eat Out
去外面吃 p.130

I passed the computer certification test.

So my family decided to eat out.

My mother drove, and our family went to a Chinese restaurant.

But the restaurant was not open yet.

My dad searched for another restaurant on his phone, and we went there.

Review Test 5 .... pp.132~133

A ① take ② talk ③ congratulate ④ listen
⑤ eat ⑥ feel ⑦ stay ⑧ paint
⑨ collect ⑩ drive ⑪ call ⑫ thank ⑬ turn
⑭ decide ⑮ give

B ① ⓕ ② ⓓ ③ ⓗ ④ ⓒ ⑤ ⓐ
⑥ ⓑ ⑦ ⓖ ⑧ ⓙ ⑨ ⓔ ⑩ ⓘ

C ① tidying up my room
② try, while
③ carring the bookshelf
④ played the violin
⑤ computer certification test

D ① I felt bored all day.
② My hobby is collecting my favorite singer's albums.
③ It took 2 hours to finish the work.
④ I gave a bouquet of flowers to my friend.
⑤ My family decided to eat out.

212

Week 6

Day 26 Go Camping
去露營 p.138

My family went camping in the valley.
I cooked dinner with my dad.
We sat around the campfire and roasted marshmallows.
We saw the moon in the night sky.
My family went to bed around 12 o'clock.

Day 27 Stationery Store
文具店 p.142

A new semester began this month.
I wanted to buy colored pencils.
I walked to the stationery store.
I asked the owner where the colored pencils were.
They were 550 NTD.
I paid 1,000 NTD and got 450 NTD back.

Day 28 Fighting with a Friend
跟朋友吵架 p.146

Today I felt bad because I had a fight with my friend.
I played baseball with my friends.
But one of them didn't follow the game rules.
I was irritated and fought with him.
Mom told me to yield and said a proverb, "A friend is a second self."
I reluctantly answered, "Yes, I will."

Day 29 New Sweater
新毛衣 p.150

My mom made me a dress.
I tried on the dress.
It looked pretty and good on me.
I took a selfie.
I uploaded it on my SNS account.
Many friends saw the photo and wrote comments.

Day 30 Math Test
數學測驗 p.154

I took a science test today.
I had no worry because I studied it hard.
But the problems were unfamiliar.
I couldn't solve all the problems in time.
In the end, I got a low score.

Review Test 6 .... pp.156~157

A 1 want 2 answer 3 look 4 fight 5 take
  6 sit 7 make 8 see 9 pay 10 get
  11 cook 12 study 13 tell

B 1 around 2 campfire 3 semester 4 owner
  5 follow 6 yield 7 selfie 8 account
  9 low 10 score

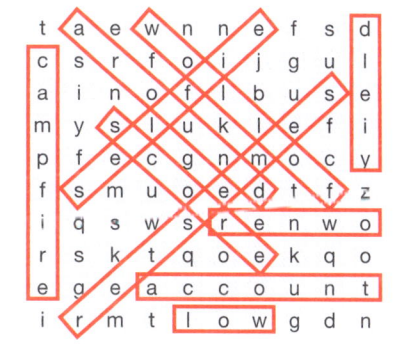

```
t a e w n n e f s d
c s r f o i j g u l
a i n o f l b u s e
m x y s l u k l e f
p f e c g n m o c y
f s m u o e d t f z
i q s w s r e n w o
r s k t q o e k q o
e g e a c c o u n t
i r m t l o w g d n
```

C 1 in the valley
  2 stationery store
  3 played baseball, friends
  4 uploaded
  5 solve all the problems

D 1 I cooked dinner with my dad.
  2 I wanted to buy a notebook.
  3 I was angry and fought with my friend.
  4 My mom made me a sweater.
  5 I took a math test today.

213

Week 7

Day 31 **Doing Housework**
　　　做家事 p.162

I was washing the dishes.
I missed a bowl and it broke.
I was embarrssed, and my mom came to me.
My mom asked me, "Are you all right?"
I said to my mom, "I'm okay."
She told me to be careful next time.

Day 32 **Math Study**
　　　念數學 p.166

I learned rectangles today.
However, I was irritated because I didn't understand the class content.
I came home and cried.
But soon, I didn't think crying would solve the problem.
I decided to review the lesson for 30 minutes every day.

Day 33 **Saving Money**
　　　存錢 p.170

I plan to go to an art exhibition.
However, the ticket price is not cheap at 500 NTD.
I don't have enough money to buy the ticket.
I'm saving up money to buy it.
I hope I can save money before the art exhibition.

Day 34 **Moving and Transferring**
　　　搬家跟轉學 p.174

My family lives in Jeonju.
We will move to Seoul next month because of my brother's career.
I also have to transfer to another school.
I'm going to miss my friends.
I will take many pictures with my friends before moving.

Day 35 **Running**
　　　跑步 p.178

Our class ran during P.E. class.
I ran quickly at the sound of a whistle.
I was running second.
Suddenly, I bumped into the friend next to me.
I fell and ended up in last place.

Review Test 7 .... pp.180~181

A ①cry ②live ③wash ④run ⑤plan
　　⑥solve ⑦understand ⑧end ⑨miss
　　⑩break ⑪move ⑫save ⑬say ⑭hope
　　⑮fall

B ①ⓓ ②ⓐ ③ⓔ ④ⓑ ⑤ⓕ
　　⑥ⓙ ⑦ⓒ ⑧ⓘ ⑨ⓖ ⑩ⓗ

C ①be careful
　　②review the lesson
　　③enough money
　　④transfer to
　　⑤ran quickly

D ①I was washing the dishes.
　　②I came home and cried.
　　③I'm saving up money to buy the ticket.
　　④My family lives in Seoul.
　　⑤I fell and ended up in last place.

Week 8

Day 36   Science Museum
科博館 p.186

Our class went to the science museum.
I chose observation of constellations among the activities.
I entered the observation room.
The observation was so exciting that I lost track of time.
I didn't know much about the universe, but today
I became interested in it.

Day 37   Lie
說謊 p.190

I hated going to the English academy.
I lied to my mom, "I have a headache."
She said to me, "If you have a severe headache,
don't go to the academy."
I thought it would feel good lying on the bed all day.
However, I felt uncomfortable because I lied.
I told her the truth and went to the academy.

Day 38   Finding the Wallet
找皮夾 p.194

I need a transportation card to go to my friend's house.
So I tried to find the card in my room.
However, my room was not tidy.
I cleaned up my room first.
I still couldn't find the card.
Suddenly, I remembered putting it inside my bag.

Day 39   Strengths of My Friend
朋友的優點 p.198

My best friend Woo-bin has many strengths.
He swims very well.
He can speak Japanese and Spanish.
He also jumps rope well.
I will try hard to become a great student like Woo-bin.

Day 40   Praise
稱讚 p.202

I drew in art class today.
I showed my picture to the teacher.
She smiled brightly and praised me.
I hung my picture at the back of the classroom.
My classmates envied me when they saw my picture.
I gained confidence in drawing.

Review Test 8 .... pp.204~205

A [1] know   [2] clean   [3] lie   [4] hate   [5] have
   [6] choose   [7] draw   [8] find   [9] speak   [10] enter
   [11] remember   [12] swim   [13] lie   [14] hang   [15] show

B [1] activity   [2] among   [3] academy   [4] severe
   [5] wallet   [6] messy   [7] strength   [8] become
   [9] shoulder   [10] envy

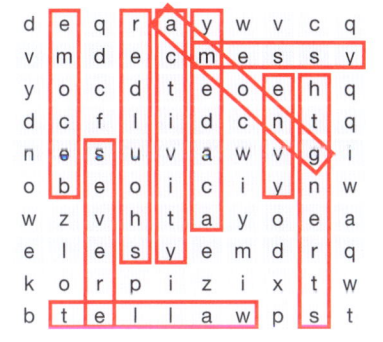

C [1] the science museum
   [2] uncomfortable
   [3] still couldn't
   [4] jumps rope
   [5] smiled brightly

D [1] I entered the theater and put on the 3D glasses.
   [2] I hated going to the math academy.
   [3] I tried to find my wallet in my room.
   [4] My best friend Min-su has many strengths.
   [5] I showed my picture to the teacher.

215

附 錄

動詞形態變化表 請仔細觀察動詞的變化形態並好好記住。

原形動詞	字義	第三人稱單數現在形	過去形	現在分詞
agree	① 同意～ ② 達成共識	agrees	agreed	agreeing
answer	① 回答 ② 回應	answers	answered	answering
arrive	抵達	arrives	arrived	arriving
ask	① 問；詢問 ② 要求；請求	asks	asked	asking
bake	烘焙（麵包等）	bakes	baked	baking
become	成為～	becomes	became	becoming
believe	相信；認為～	believes	believed	believing
borrow	① 借入（物品） ② 借入（錢）	borrows	borrowed	borrowing
break	① 打破，打碎；弄壞 ② 破裂；壞掉，故障	breaks	broke	breaking
buy	① 購買 ② 買給～	buys	bought	buying
call	① 呼叫；喊叫 ② 打電話	calls	called	calling
catch	① 抓住 ② 趕上	catches	caught	catching
change	① 更換 ② 兌換	changes	changed	changing
choose	① 選擇 ② 選取	chooses	chose	choosing
clean	打掃；清潔	cleans	cleaned	cleaning
climb	攀登；爬上	climbs	climbed	climbing
collect	收集；使集合	collects	collected	collecting
come	來	comes	came	coming
congratulate	恭喜	congratulates	congratulated	congratulating
cook	料理，烹飪	cooks	cooked	cooking
cry	① 哭泣 ② 喊叫	cries	cried	crying

原形動詞	字義	第三人稱單數現在形	過去形	現在分詞
dance	① 跳舞 ② 跳（特定的舞步）	dances	danced	dancing
decide	決定	decides	decided	deciding
die	死亡	dies	died	dying
discuss	討論（關於～）	discusses	discussed	discussing
draw	① 劃（線）；畫（圖） ② 拖；拉 ③（在比賽中）打成平手	draws	drew	drawing
drink	喝	drinks	drank	drinking
drive	① 駕駛 ② 用車載送（人）	drives	drove	driving
eat	吃	eats	ate	eating
end	① 結束 ② 終止	ends	ended	ending
enter	① 進入；進去 ② 入學；參加	enters	entered	entering
exercise	① 運動 ② 鍛鍊；操練	exercises	exercised	exercising
fail	失敗；（在考試中）沒有通過或不及格	fails	failed	failing
fall	① 倒下，跌倒 ② 掉落	falls	fell	falling
feel	① 感受（情緒等） ②（透過觸摸來）感受	feels	felt	feeling
fight	打架；爭吵	fights	fought	fighting
find	① 找到；發現 ② 意識到；發覺	finds	found	finding
fly	① 飛 ② 飛行	flies	flew	flying
forget	忘記；忘了	forgets	forgot	forgetting
get	① 收到 ② 得到	gets	got	getting
give	給	gives	gave	giving
go	去	goes	went	going

原形動詞	字義	第三人稱單數現在形	過去形	現在分詞
grow	① 生長；發育 ② 栽培，種植	grows	grew	growing
hang	① 懸掛；吊起 ② 掛著，吊著	hangs	hung	hanging
hate	討厭	hates	hated	hating
have	① 有 ② 得到（疾病等） ③ 擁有（時間等） ④ 擁有（身體或心理上的特質） ⑤ 吃；喝	has	had	having
help	① 幫助 ② 取用（食物等）	helps	helped	helping
hold	① 握著；抓住 ② 保持	holds	held	holding
hope	希望	hopes	hoped	hoping
hurry	趕緊；匆忙	hurries	hurried	hurrying
introduce	① 介紹 ② 推出	introduces	introduced	introducing
invite	邀請	invites	invited	inviting
know	知道；了解	knows	knew	knowing
learn	學；學習	learns	learned	learning
lie	說謊	lies	lied	lying
lie	① 躺 ② 呈現（某種狀態）	lies	lay	lying
listen	① 聆聽 ② 聽從	listens	listened	listening
live	居住；生活	lives	lived	living
look	① 看 ② 看起來	looks	looked	looking
love	① 熱愛 ② 喜歡（做～）	loves	loved	loving
make	① 做；製造 ② 使～做～	makes	made	making
meet	遇到；碰面	meets	met	meeting

原形動詞	字義	第三人稱單數現在形	過去形	現在分詞
miss	① 想念 ② 錯過	misses	missed	missing
move	① 搬遷；移動 ② 搬動	moves	moved	moving
need	① 需要 ② 有必要做～	needs	needed	needing
open	① 打開～ ② 開	opens	opened	opening
paint	油漆；塗上顏色	paints	painted	painting
pay	支付	pays	paid	paying
pick	① 挑選；選擇 ② 摘 ③ 撿	picks	picked	picking
plan	① 計劃；打算（做某件事） ② 制定計畫，規劃	plans	planned	planning
play	① 玩耍 ②（和～）比賽；進行（遊戲或運動） ③ 演奏	plays	played	playing
practice	練習	practices	practiced	practicing
read	① 閱讀 ② 寫明；標明	reads	read	reading
record	記錄；錄製（聲音或影像等內容）	records	recorded	recording
remember	記得，想起	remembers	remembered	remembering
return	① 歸還 ② 返回	returns	returned	returning
run	跑；跑步	runs	ran	running
save	① 存～ ② 拯救，挽救	saves	saved	saving
say	說	says	said	saying
score	得分	scores	scored	scoring
see	① 看見，看到 ② 理解，知道	sees	saw	seeing

原形動詞	字義	第三人稱單數現在形	過去形	現在分詞
sell	① 賣 ② 售出	sells	sold	selling
send	發送；寄送；傳送	sends	sent	sending
show	顯現；給～看	shows	showed	showing
sing	① 唱歌 ② 唱（某首歌）	sings	sang	singing
sit	坐	sits	sat	sitting
smell	① 發出味道 ② 聞味道	smells	smelled	smelling
solve	解決；解答	solves	solved	solving
speak	說	speaks	spoke	speaking
start	① 開始，著手 ② 開始 ③ 出發	starts	started	starting
stay	暫留；停留	stays	stayed	staying
study	學習	studies	studied	studying
swim	游泳	swims	swam	swimming
take	① 抓 ② 吃（藥） ③ 採取（行動） ④ 搭乘（交通工具） ⑤ 花費（時間等） ⑥ 參加（考試） ⑦ 拍攝（照片）	takes	took	taking
talk	說話；談論	talks	talked	talking
tell	說；告訴；吩咐	tells	told	telling
thank	感謝	thanks	thanked	thanking
think	思考；認為；想	thinks	thought	thinking
try	① 試圖；努力 ② 嘗試	tries	tried	trying
turn	① 轉向 ② 使轉動	turns	turned	turning
understand	理解，懂得	understands	understood	understanding

原形動詞	字義	第三人稱單數現在形	過去形	現在分詞
visit	① 探望；拜訪 ② 訪問（網站等）	visits	visited	visiting
wait	等待	waits	waited	waiting
wake	① 清醒；醒來 ② 喚醒	wakes	woke	waking
walk	行走	walks	walked	walking
want	① 要 ② 想要 ③ 希望	wants	wanted	wanting
wash	① 清洗；洗澡 ② 洗衣服	washes	washed	washing
watch	① 觀看；注視 ② 警戒	watches	watched	watching
win	贏得；獲勝	wins	won	winning

台灣廣廈 國際出版集團
Taiwan Mansion International Group

國家圖書館出版品預行編目（CIP）資料

1本就通！小學生英文寫作力養成書/鄭孝准著；許竹瑩譯.
-- 初版. -- 新北市：國際學村出版社, 2025.05
　　面；　公分
ISBN 978-986-454-417-2(平裝)

1.CST: 英語教學 2.CST: 寫作法 3.CST: 小學教學

523.318　　　　　　　　　　　　　　　　　114003272

🌐 國際學村

1本就通！小學生英文寫作力養成書

作　　　　者／鄭孝准	編輯中心編輯長／伍峻宏
譯　　　　者／許竹瑩	編輯／徐淳輔
	封面設計／林珈仔・內頁排版／菩薩蠻數位文化有限公司
	製版・印刷・裝訂／東豪・弼聖・秉成

行企研發中心總監／陳冠蒨　　　線上學習中心總監／陳冠蒨
媒體公關組／陳柔彣　　　　　　企製開發組／張哲剛
綜合業務組／何欣穎

發　行　人／江媛珍
法　律　顧　問／第一國際法律事務所 余淑杏律師・北辰著作權事務所 蕭雄淋律師
出　　　　版／國際學村
發　　　　行／台灣廣廈有聲圖書有限公司
　　　　　　　地址：新北市235中和區中山路二段359巷7號2樓
　　　　　　　電話：（886）2-2225-5777・傳真：（886）2-2225-8052

讀者服務信箱／cs@booknews.com.tw

代理印務・全球總經銷／知遠文化事業有限公司
　　　　　　　地址：新北市222深坑區北深路三段155巷25號5樓
　　　　　　　電話：（886）2-2664-8800・傳真：（886）2-2664-8801

郵　政　劃　撥／劃撥帳號：18836722
　　　　　　　劃撥戶名：知遠文化事業有限公司（※單次購書金額未達1000元，請另付70元郵資。）

■出版日期：2025年05月　　ISBN：978-986-454-417-2
　　　　　　　　　　　　　　版權所有，未經同意不得重製、轉載、翻印。

초등 영어일기 쓰기
Copyright © 2024 by Jung Hyo Jun
All rights reserved.
Original Korean edition published by Saramin.
Chinese(complex) Translation rights arranged with Saramin.
Chinese(complex) Translation Copyright © 2025 by Taiwan Mansion Publishing Co.,
Ltd. through M.J. Agency, in Taipei.